WHITE PINE

WHITE PINE

American History and the Tree That Made a Nation

ANDREW VIETZE

Globe
Pequot

Guilford, Connecticut

Globe
Pequot

An imprint of Rowman & Littlefield

Distributed by NATIONAL BOOK NETWORK

British Library Cataloguing in Publication Information available

Library of Congress Cataloging-in-Publication Data available

ISBN 978-1-4930-0907-7 (paperback)
ISBN 978-1-4930-2331-8 (e-book)

∞™ The paper used in this publication meets the minimum requirements of American National Standard for Information Sciences—Permanence of Paper for Printed Library Materials, ANSI/NISO Z39.48-1992.

Printed in the United States of America

Thanks go to my wife and two boys, who let me live among the pines, and to my parents for introducing them to me in the first place.

Contents

Preface

Between every two pine trees there is a door leading to a new way of life.

—John Muir[1]

When I was a boy, I used to walk from tree to tree high above the forest floor, clinging to pitchy pine branches, feet on a bough like a tightrope walker. At the time, we lived forty-five minutes southwest of Boston in a venerable cape built in 1720, with secret alcoves to escape native attacks and, more importantly to me, acres of woods out back. In the small forest backyard was a grove of towering, majestic eastern white pines that jutted far above the tree line, all twisting and arcing. Hundreds of feet tall and too fat for me to wrap my arms around, they were gathered together like some superior order, commanding the neighborhood. Somehow the noble conifers escaped the suburbanization that went on all around them, the growth for growth's sake that would see streets of identical houses built in every direction for miles and eventually send my family packing—to the Pine Tree State.

I loved those trees.

They were my refuge.

In one was my "tree fort," little more than a platform of boards twenty feet up, where I would sit and play for hours. Sometimes I'd simply lean back against its trunk and read. Other times I'd listen to the wind faintly whisper through the needles as the wind blew, as if it had secrets it wanted to share with me. Sometimes it was make believe Star Wars with my cousin, holding on to the tree like an Ewok of Endor; other times it was a haven from an angry sibling or yelling parent. Often I'd watch the sun go down off to the west and reluctantly climb down to go inside. And then there were those rare moments when I'd hang on and walk through the canopy from one tree to the next, looking down at the rust-red floor of the forest below.

I loved those trees.

My favorite place, though, was up in Maine, where we'd spend a week every summer visiting with family on a peninsula that reached out into one of the Midcoast's many tidal rivers. Once a saltwater farm where my grandmother spent her childhood, our ancestral plot was mostly wide-open meadow, but as you got closer to the water, a narrow forest of pine and oak clung to the riverbank. In those woods were several giant white pines, and they made the same magic sound when the wind blew, filled with their own secrets. They provided us with shade on hot July days, looked over countless family picnics, held a swing that amused generations of us, and wore a carved wooden sign that told us we'd arrived.

I loved those trees, too.

Today, I work as a ranger in one of the nation's last great wilderness areas, a proud member of the thin green line, protecting the park from the people and the people from the park (mostly the former). My duty station? An old sporting camp that used to be called Twin Pines, for the skyscraping pair of white pine towers that frame a jaw-dropping view of Maine's greatest mountain.

Fifteen feet around, seventy-five feet tall, they must be two hundred years old, witness to centuries of lumbering and hunting and now hiking and paddling. Every year they drop giant cones the size of bananas. And lose branches that could take out a car.

The eastern white pine has served as the backdrop of my life. And all of these trees have seen a lot.

The stories they could tell.

Before I began this project, I had no idea exactly how much they'd witnessed. I didn't know how important they'd been to the native peoples, literally keeping them alive during some particularly brutal winters. Or how valuable they were to King James I, who saw in them a way to build the world's best navy and dominate a continent. Or to the colonists, for whom they became a symbol of revolution. I didn't know that a riot in New Hampshire, which began over the cutting of pines, was the inspiration for the much more famous Boston Tea Party. Or that the rebels saw the tree as so central a theme in the build-up to war that they sewed it onto the flags they carried to the Battle of Bunker Hill. Or that the Massachusetts State House in Boston had sculpted pine cones on its dome, a symbol of the integral role the tree played in New England's development. I was unaware how much the pine meant to the early builders of America. And I had no idea about the value the tree still has to the economy today, whether in the form of boards for building or in the potions and tinctures that herbalists use to cure our many ailments.

I just knew I loved those trees.

This book doesn't purport to be a comprehensive history of the eastern white pine. I told a group of young writing students at a workshop last year that there's no excuse for academic writing, and I'm a man of my word. Besides, who wants to read a doorstop about a tree? Instead it's intended to be a collection of stories about this magnificent species and the profound impact they've had on our world.

It's my attempt to tell the stories they were always trying to whisper to me.

Introduction: White Pine Riot

The only reason why the Rebellion at Portsmouth and the "Boston Tea Party" are better known than our Pine Tree Riot is because they have had better historians.
                                        —William Little[1]

The intruders held the Hillsborough County Sheriff spread-eagled, suspended above the floor of his bed chamber, face down. More than twenty of them gathered around him—two on each side gripped fast as the others looked on—their faces painted black with soot. The lawman struggled against them, eyes wide, feet thrashing, kicking over the lamp on the bedside table and sending bedding flying, but they only tightened their hold, resolute underneath their macabre makeup and too numerous to escape.

Dawn's first rays were just beginning to glow on the walls of Sheriff Benjamin Whiting's room at the Aaron Quimby Inn, in Weare, New Hampshire, when the black-faced men burst through the door. The constable had been asleep but he woke with a start and dove for his guns; the large group easily prevented him from reaching them. They jerked him from his four-poster, stripped the bedclothes off his torso, and wrenched him over so that his naked back faced the ceiling.

Men on each limb clutched Whiting tightly, holding him at waist height, while others brought out the switches. With the snap of a whip but the heft of a stick, the sharp saplings were ideal for what they had in mind, and as the sheriff struggled, rocking to try and pull himself free, the men laid into him, whipping him on the sides and back, keeping at it until he was a raw mess, flesh hanging down, blood dripping onto the rug below. Then they used the sharpened tips of the sticks to dig hash marks into his back—each representing a fine the men owed—and dumped him to the floor. As Whiting would say later: "They almost killed me."[2]

Down the hall, another group, similarly disguised, was doing the same to Whiting's deputy, John Quigley. Quigley put up more of a fight, however—and consequently got more of a beating, the men subduing him with repeated whacks from "long poles."[3]

After making their point, the attackers hauled their two bloody captives outside, where the lawmen had left their horses. During the night, the men in blackened faces had shaved the manes and tails and cut the ears of each animal, greatly reducing their value with a few snips—and making them look ridiculous in the process. Pine boughs tied into their fur here and there added to the effect. Sheriff and deputy were hefted onto their motley mounts, facing backwards, and tied in place with rawhide lashes. Then their clothes were thrown at them—these townspeople were no thieves—and the horses were sent cantering down the Mast Road with a slap on the rump to the "jeers" and "jokes"[4] of all who had gathered at the inn on Eastman Hill.

Benjamin Whiting hadn't expected this rough treatment when he rode into Weare the previous day, April 13, 1772. The very first sheriff of Hillsborough County—the district had only just organized the year before—he had packed his pistols, but he always carried them when he went to enforce King George's laws. In remote places like this woods hamlet, rebellious sentiments seemed to fortify the drinking water. Located sixteen miles southwest of Concord, Weare had originally been called Beverly-Canada, and much of its land had been settled by veterans of the French and Indian Wars, who had received parcels as payments for their service. The village was still little more than a couple of inns and a smattering of sawmills, and it had been just eight years since it changed its name to Weare, to honor the town clerk, Meshech Weare. Pines climbed the heights of Mount Dearborn, Mine Hill, and Mount Wallingford, each of which crested at about a thousand feet and spread across all the hillocks and rises beneath. These woods were the area's primary industry.

Sheriff Whiting had ridden into countless communities like this as a proud, loyal representative of an unpopular monarch. He'd personally been threatened on several occasions—the worst was probably that September night in Brattleboro, Vermont, in 1769, when he was transporting a trio of prisoners back to Albany. Then, Whiting had been lodged upstairs in a log home when a "riotous number of men"[5] broke in and demanded he release his captives, timber cutters Willard and William Deane. When he refused, the mob spent the night issuing "many violent threats"[6] against his life. He barely managed to escape the next morning with the outlaws in tow. The men under arrest that night were to be tried for the same crime that had brought Whiting to Weare— felling the king's pines.

By contrast to that night in Brattleboro, however, his errand in Weare looked like it was going to be relatively simple. He'd come to the village to serve a warrant for the arrest of mill owner Ebenezer Mudgett, who, along with several other townsmen, had been caught illegally helping themselves to the king's pines, the finest trees in the forest.

The law was clear: Every eastern white pine tall enough and straight enough to be the mast of a ship had been proclaimed the property of the King of England in the Massachusetts Bay Colony Charter of 1691. In 1722, the New Hampshire General Court had followed Massachusetts's lead, enacting the law for their own woodlands, ceding the forest's finest to King George I. "ALL trees of the diameter of 24 inches and upward of 12 inches from the ground" were to be considered royal goods, and every winter Sherriff Whiting and other representatives of the crown walked the woods, selecting pines and marking them with the hated broad arrow—three cuts of a hatchet in the shape of a point. Cutting a king's pine would cost the perpetrator five pounds and perhaps even a few nights in jail.

Since first sighting them in the seventeenth century, the English had been obsessed with the evergreens they found in their North American colonies. When they discovered the fastness of New England, where eastern white pines grew long and straight and rolled off to every horizon, raising their crowns high above the tree line, their limbs splayed against the sky as if drawn by a calligrapher's brush, trundling across mountains and valleys and covering the land as far as the eye could see, they were quick to claim them. Tall and strong, relatively long-lasting, able to bend without snapping, these noble evergreens made just the sort of masts to fly the sails and flags of the world's greatest navy. The sky-scraping, two-hundred-foot timbers were unlike anything that could be found in the British Isles, where the tallest trees had been swept down centuries before.

The English navy—then the most powerful armada on earth—badly needed a constant, reliable source of naval stores, including lumber for their ships' masts. Before they found the North American conifer, the Royal Navy had to cobble together masts out of two or more trunks from the forests of eastern Europe, and the joining greatly reduced their strength. Worse, they had to trust that mast material could make it from the slopes of the Baltics all the way to the port of London, through waters infested with Dutch and French privateers. The New England pines were strong and stout and the perfect height for masts. Each one alone could become a single spar.

By the mid-eighteenth century, however, New England residents were cutting the king's pines where and when they pleased—from Connecticut to the Maine coast—milling the wood and selling it for boards to build homes that were sprouting up like dandelions along the roads spreading out from Boston. The colonists—quickly earning the designation "traitorous rebels" from the English—considered the trees rightfully theirs, crucial to their economic livelihoods and to their very way of life, regardless of the law. The image of a pine tree had been sewn onto their flags as far back as 1686 as a symbol of New England. They had printed the evergreens on their currency—the Massachusetts Bay colony had "tree money," six-pence coins that showed a pine, dating back to 1652. They considered the noble evergreen an icon of liberty and put it on banners and pamphlets supporting the rights of the colony. However, as rebellion began to foment in New England in the years leading up to the Revolutionary War, pine, like sugar and tea and stamps, marked with the "broad arrow" had become an example of the king's tyranny. Increasingly, the colonists scoffed at the notion that a monarch 3,279 miles across the sea owned trees quite literally in their backyards. Instead, they adhered to their own "Swamp Law." Under it, they cut the best and most regal pines for themselves and then carved broad arrows into tiny trees in mockery. They pointed with pride at their pine floorboards, which were considerably wider than the twenty-four inches allowed under law.

Initially, the king's enforcement efforts were indifferent to this, and British authorities paid logging outlaws little heed. The woods were vast and the problems were often in areas too remote to worry about. And the Brits only had a few men to cover thousands of miles. They occasionally clamped down, though, as when the king's surveyor general, David Dunbar, burned the homes of sawyers in Sheepscot, Province of Maine, in 1730. But it wasn't until John Wentworth became governor of New Hampshire in 1766 that surveyors were regularly dispatched to the woods to search for illegal timbers. The governor even led the inspections himself, transported by a driver to mills across the region. From one end of New England to the other, men were fined and arrested for felling the king's pines, and nowhere was the problem more prevalent than New Hampshire. A sweep done in the winter of 1771–1772 found illegal logs at mills in Goffstown and in Weare, where mill owners were labeled "notorious offenders"[7] by the governor. More than 270 pines between seventeen and thirty-six inches wide and clearly bearing the mark of the broad arrow were discovered at Clements Mill at the Oil Mill Village in South Weare, and many more were found at sawyers in nearby Bedford.

Because of the extent of the crimes there, these communities were chosen as places to set an example, to impose the will of the king. Just a few weeks before Sherriff Whiting was accosted by residents of Weare, the February 7, 1772, edition of the *New Hampshire Gazette* reported that mill owner Ebenezer Mudgett and a few others had been charged with the crime of cutting the king's pines, and that proceedings had begun at the Court of Vice Admiralty in Portsmouth. The lawyer retained by the sawyers encouraged the men to simply pay their fines and be done with it, and several of the men from Goffstown and Bedford elected to do so.

Ebenezer Mudgett did not.

When Sheriff Whiting and Deputy John Quigley, of Francestown, arrived in Weare that April, they had found Mudgett easily enough and served him his warrant, meeting him at the aptly named Pine Tree Tavern at Aaron Quimby's Inn, where the first barrel of rum in Weare had arrived years before and where "the old loggerhead was always kept at a white heat." Sheriff Benjamin Whiting had delivered many a warrant to such outlaws, and he was working on the assumption that if he locked up Ebenezer Mudgett, the most prominent of the mill owners in Weare, the others who had outstanding fines would simply pay up to avoid arrest. As they sat in the inn, perhaps over a three-pence mug of Quimby's famous "flip," a drink made of rum, apple, bran, and pumpkin, they discussed Mudgett's options. He could cooperate and pay his fine or be manacled and taken back to Exeter for processing.

Mudgett seemed amenable enough, and he told the king's men he'd come back in the morning with his "bail" money. Whiting and Quigley repaired to their rooms at the inn that evening, quite pleased at how simple it had been to serve the warrant, joking with one another that these mill owners were just a lot of "hoodlums with no more spine than rabbits."[8]

Then came the dawn, when the black-faced men burst through the sheriff's door at the inn and tore him from his bed.

Days after his beating, Whiting enlisted the help of a British colonel named Moore and returned to Weare with a large contingent of armed men to confront Mudgett and his cronies. Neither Mudgett nor any of his coconspirators could be found. Storming around town, the sheriff eventually discovered one of the men, who ratted out the others. When they were found, all were charged with rioting, disturbing the peace, and "making an assault upon the body of Benjamin Whiting."[9] Eight men from Weare went to trial in the case—Ebenezer Mudgett, Timothy Worthley, Jonathan Worthley, Caleb Atwood, William Dustin, Abraham Johnson, Jonathan Tuttle, and William Quimby, whose brother owned the inn. They were arraigned, and each pleaded guilty at a hearing at the Superior Court in Amherst in September 1772, standing before four judges. Though they had the widespread support of their New England neighbors who were fed up with the British and their policies, each man ended up paying twenty shillings plus the cost of the hearing for their crimes.

Later dubbed the Pine Tree Riot, the incident at the Aaron Quimby Inn was among the first acts of violence against representatives of the British crown by disaffected colonists, and some say it was the inspiration for another event that would occur twenty months later alongside Boston Harbor, where face-painted men told the king what he could do with his policies, ceremoniously upending caskets of tea into the briny. Soon the English-appointed governors in New England would find that a band of tree-cutting rebels were but one small part of their problem, and loyalists like

Sheriff Whiting would begin fleeing towns across New England. In 1778, Benjamin Whiting himself was banished as a Tory and his property was seized by New Hampshire rebels.

The riots and revolts escalated across Massachusetts until the fateful day when the British discovered the colonists had a cache of munitions stored in Concord, Massachusetts, and marched there to capture both the weapons and two of the primary rabble rousers, Samuel Adams and John Hancock. On their way there, at Lexington, English authorities found just how aggrieved the people of New England felt—about their trees and their stamps and taxes and their tea—and musket balls began to fly.

And in June 1775, when the colonists met the British at the Battle of Bunker Hill, they did so under a new flag. Featured prominently in the upper left-hand corner of the red banner, dark green against a white backdrop, was the image of a white pine.

CHAPTER ONE

The Bark Eaters

*Can you hear the dreams crackling like a campfire? Can you
hear the dreams sweeping through the pine trees and tipis?*
                                        —SHERMAN ALEXIE[1]

NEW YORK, NEW YORK, NOVEMBER 28, 2013. THE MACY'S
Thanksgiving Day Parade, in its eighty-seventh year, trundled up
the Avenue of the Americas. Millions lined the street, staring up at
Snoopy and Woodstock, SpongeBob and Buzz Lightyear and the
freakish Elf on the Shelf. Jimmy Fallon mugged with Cookie Monster while Cirque du Soleil did head-spinning tricks. The Duck
Dynasty clan waved from beneath their beards aboard the *Marion
Carole*, a replica paddlewheeler and the largest showboat to ever
float the parade route. Overhead, Ronald McDonald looked down
with a lipstick leer, and a grim-faced Uncle Sam gave a thumbs-up.
Old rockers the Goo Goo Dolls shilled chocolate for Lindt, and the
ageless Richard Simmons glided by on the back of a turtle. A classic
Thanksgiving tradition, the parade was loud and brash and colorful,
an advertiser's subliminal dream, all a bit surreal.

And, of course, as American as it got.

That year, it was more deeply American than many of the
millions watching even knew. Among the sixteen hundred cheer-
leaders, eleven marching bands, fifty-two balloons,[2] and dozens

of smiling celebrities was another turtle float, this one truck sized, depicting a colorful reptile, its shell all swirling circles, with its legs splayed out in four directions. On the animal's back was a thirty-foot white pine, roots clinging to the carapace, with a bald eagle in its uppermost branches. Native Americans dressed in traditional garb smiled and waved from balconies located around the float, while others danced in the street. A skirt of wampum beads wrapped around the base of the float interrupted by a big shield that read "Oneida Indian Nation."

These were the First Americans, and the float—the first ever sponsored by an Indian nation—was called "The True Spirit of Thanksgiving." The Oneida—originally from upstate New York—wasn't the tribe that celebrated with the Pilgrims at the first Thanksgiving, of course (that would be the Wampanoags). But with this float they gave thanks to something larger than that fraternal feast. In fact, "True Spirit of Thanksgiving" represented the "oldest tradition" of the Iroquois Nation, to which the Oneida belong.

The Oneida explained the float's design this way: "On the Turtle's back (known as Turtle Island) stands a White Pine Tree. The roots that spread out from the tree are called the Great Roots of Peace, and they spread in the four directions: one to the north, one to the south, one to the east, and one to the west. On top of this Great Tree is placed an Eagle. The Eagle keeps a watchful eye on the roots and if any danger approaches, he will scream loudly, sounding the alarm."[3]

The majestic white pine was an elemental part of many Native American cultures, but it was especially sacred to the Iroquois, the people of the Five Nations. To the Oneida, Cayuga, Seneca, Mohawk, and Onandaga, the resinous conifer represented salvation from years of bloodshed and war. It symbolized brotherhood, harmony, even survival. Just as the tree was at the center of the turtle's back, it sat at the center of the Five Nation's creation story.

Peter Jemison, caretaker of Ganondagan, a New York State historical park and sacred place of the Seneca, and native Seneca himself, explains:

Initially the Five Nations were warring against themselves. There was continuous fighting—people sometimes refer to it as blood feuds—between families and between nations. It was a chaotic, dangerous time to be alive. It was a time of great sorrow with people living in fear of each other.

The story goes that, watching from above, the Creator was disturbed by all of the hatred and violence. "We always say that the Creator took pity on us and sent us a messenger of peace," says Jemison.

Called simply the Peacemaker, the prophet sent by the Creator was a Huron named Deganawidah, who traveled among all the tribes of the Great Lakes region, bringing with him a new law from the Creator. Some tribes challenged him, others accepted him warmly, and two people helped him. One was a Mohawk brave named Hiawatha ("not the same one from the Longfellow poem," says Jemison). The other was a Seneca woman, whose word carried great weight in the native society, which was both matrilineal and reverential of elders. "We call her, in English, the Mother of All Nations," says Jemison. "She was the first to give women the rights they now have."

After many adventures and trials—and with the assistance of the pair—the Peacemaker convinced leaders of the five tribes to gather for a meeting beneath a soaring eastern white pine. According to tradition, the iconic tree had wide arms, to provide shelter, and an enormous underpinning, just like the one on the Oneida float. "Four roots grew under the tree in the four cardinal directions," Jemison explains. "The tribes' weapons were placed under the tree and floated away on an underground stream.

And the bloodletting ceased. As the Peacemaker advanced his message, the symbol he chose was the White Pine," says Jemison, "because its needles come in clusters of five—like the Five Nations—and because the tree was evergreen and continued to grow even in winter. It was seen as eternal, like the confederacy he was trying to build."

The meeting under the tree led to the creation of a sophisticated system of governance that kept the peace—and kept the tribes united—through the centuries of trial and war that were to come. What had been five disparate warring peoples transformed into one of the most powerful forces in the northeast of North America in the seventeenth and eighteenth centuries.

When the Europeans arrived, the French called the five tribes the Iroquois. The English called them the Five Nation Confederacy. "We called ourselves the 'Haudenosaunee,'" Jemison says, a name that meant "people of the long house." "The Seneca guarded the western door. The Cayuga, Oneida, and Onandonga kept the central fires burning, and the Mohawk guarded the eastern door." (Eventually the Tuscarora were invited to join and became a sixth tribe.)

An ardent tribal historian, Jemison conducted an oral history with his people, asking elders how long ago and where this meeting was said to have to have occurred. "Many said it happened over a thousand years ago," he says. "They had heard the story in their native language passed down to them. I also spoke to others who said it might even have been two thousand years ago." Other historians and anthropologists date the origins of the confederacy to 1142, 1450, and 1600. Neither tribal leaders nor anthropologists are sure where the Great Tree of Peace was located, but there are stories that shed light on possible sites. Jemison tells the story of a visit the Peacemaker paid to the Mohawk. "When he first spoke to the Mohawk they tested him. They made him climb a tree—it could have been a white pine. It was described as a very tall tree on the edge of a cliff above a waterfall. They said they would cut it down [as he was in it], and if he survived the fall they would know he was telling the truth. And he did survive." That site is generally believed to be at Cohoes Falls in western New York.

Other sites from the tale have also been identified. Onandaga Lake in central New York State, where the Onandaga tradition- ally gathered, became known as the location of the central fire. Ganondagan, the site where Jemison works, was the home of the largest Seneca town, a place of more than 150 houses before it was destroyed in a French raid in 1687, and it's a sacred ground believed to be the home of the Mother of All Nations and a white pine Tree of Peace.

The eastern white pine became a revered symbol used in many Iroquois ceremonies, some that Jemison won't even talk about. "It has a more sacred nature that we don't go in to [with people out- side the tribe]." Anthropologist Arthur C. Parker spent some time studying Iroquois culture and reveals some of these traditions in his essay "Certain Iroquois Tree Myths and Symbols." He refers to the white pine as the Seneca "World Tree."

> *This tree is mentioned in various ceremonial rites of the Iro-*
> *quois. With the False Face Company, Hadïgo^n'sä sho^n'o^n, for*
> *example, the Great Face, chief of all the False Faces, is said*
> *to be the invisible giant that guards the world tree (gain-*
> *dowä'ně). He rubs his turtle-shell rattle upon it to obtain its*
> *power, and this he imparts to all the visible false-faces worn*
> *by the company. In visible token of this belief the members*
> *of the company rub their turtle rattles on pine-tree trunks,*
> *believing that thereby they become imbued with both the*
> *earth-power and the sky-power.*[4]

Many other tribes shared the Iroquois' reverence for *Pinus strobus*, the pitchy evergreen that towers above all other trees in the forests of the northeast. Quick growing, strong, resilient, the eastern white pine earned its name well—it's native only to North America, with a range that stretches from Newfoundland to Georgia and only as far west as the Boundary Waters of Minnesota—as easterly as it gets. A million-square-mile triangle where it finds the dry soil and cool temperatures that it favors.

And almost every tribe within that territory had a relationship with the tree in one form or another. Some celebrated the great green conifer almost as much as the Iroquois, placing it at the very beginning of their worlds. The Abenaki of Maine and the Canadian Maritimes tell of Glooscap, often regarded as their Creator, a wandering giant who came from the sky to the land where the sun rose. He paddled his canoe along the shore of North America and "turned it into a granite isle covered in spruce and pine."

Likewise, the Menominee, a people of Wisconsin, have a playful character in their folklore called Manabozho, who created the land. The story goes that he found himself at odds with vengeful spirits that lived in the lakes, and they killed his son. When Manabozho took his revenge, these aqueous demons hunted him "in the shape of a vast flood."[5] He fled, running as fast as he could up a mountain, and the water climbed up after him. Ever upwards he went, and the rising waters followed, until he'd climbed to the summit of the peak. There, he found a towering white pine, and scaled it to escape the flood. The tree grew beneath him, raising him high above the floodplain, but then it stopped. The water quickly caught back up, and Manabozho had to implore the beaver, otter, and muskrat to help him by diving to the bottom and bringing up earth to vanquish the water. Thus, with the help of a tall white pine and some furry friends, he created land.

Even when it wasn't at the center of genesis, the pine featured heavily in many native myths and traditions. The Micmac, of maritime Canada, have a story about the very first pine, which was again created by the great magician Glooscap. He promised to grant the wish of any brave warriors who could make it to his magic island in the clouds. Three brothers overcame all trials placed before them, climbing a sheer mountain of iron, past two giant serpents, and clambering under the crushing Wall of Death to reach his lodge. Glooscap was impressed, and he kept his promise, hearing their desires.

The first brother was tall and vain and wished to be even taller to attract more squaws. To that end, he wore a soaring turkey feather atop his head. The second brother wanted to stay forever in the forest, taking in its great beauty, and never having to work. And the third brother asked to live to a very old age and remain in perfect health. Glooscap turned each one into a pine tree. The first brother became the tallest pine on earth, rising high above the forest canopy, with winds whistling around him. The second brother was rooted deeply in the ground so he had to forever remain in the forest and couldn't work, and the third lived a very long life in perfect health just as he wished. As Frances Jenkins Olcott puts it in *The Red Indian Fairy Book*, "And if you go into the forest, you may see the tallest Pine Tree with his Turkey feather waving in the wind; and the Tree murmurs all day long, in the Indian tongue:

"Oh! I am such a great Indian! — Oh! I am such a tall man!"[6]

Another folktale from the Chippewa of Michigan, Wisconsin, and Minnesota similarly anthropomorphizes the tree. They tell of a legendary native maiden named Leelinau who did not like the marriage her parents arranged for her and ran away to the woods. She stopped to rest in a grove of pines, under which lived some sprites, and she leaned against a pine, confiding out loud what she'd done. "Be my wife, maiden, beautiful Leelinau, beautiful Leelinau,"[7] said a voice that seemed to be coming from the tree. In her sadness, Leelinau agreed to marry the pine tree. Her parents, worried, sent out search parties looking for her, but they never found her, and she never returned home. And it's said that hunters who venture near a certain tree would sometimes catch a glimpse of a beautiful maiden with a handsome young man, but they'd vanish upon approach.

Spend any time gazing up a towering white pine, and it's not difficult to understand why natives held the tree in such reverence. In most of the northeast, it's the tallest tree by a significant margin, a true giant of the land, marrying earth and sky. The loftiest white pines, like those at Cook Forest State Park in Pennsylvania, can scrape the sky at 170 feet, and they lord over the forest canopy, noble and powerful. Graceful and beautiful, with arms splayed out wide in welcome, *Pinus strobus* smells clean and good. And the wind makes it sing in whispers—with a good breeze, pine boughs sound almost like a distant sea. Add to all this the myriad uses the natives found for the tree and its mythic status is understandable.

The Algonquin of the northeast had particularly close ties to the eastern white pine, so much so that their ancient enemies the Mohawk used to spit the word "rondak" at them with the utmost derision. In the Mohawk language it meant "bark eater," and it poked fun at the fact that, to stave off scurvy, and to get through a few rough winters, the Algonquin would peel the bark of the eastern white pine and eat the inner layer. They also used to make a restorative tea with the needles. When the English arrived, they borrowed the word and applied it to a mountain region, only they made it easier to pronounce for their own white tongue—Adirondack.

The Algonquin weren't the only tribes to eat pine—even tribes within the Mohawks' own Iroquois Confederacy were known to munch on the shoots of infant trees. The Ojibwa used the young staminate catkins as a flavoring with stewed meat. They also ate lichen that they found at the base of white pines, boiling it until it was "like scrambled eggs."[8] The Micmac grated the inner bark and ate it to combat scurvy.

In fact, there were few parts of the tree that the natives didn't use. According to tribal historian Johnie Leverett, the Algonquin called the white pine "grandfather"[9] because it was seen as a provider. They used the trees not only as food but as shelter and medicine. When they had colds, the Algonquin boiled pine needles as an antihistamine, and they made a poultice of the inner bark to apply to the chest.

As much as the Mohawks made fun, they used the inner bark for the same purpose. Many tribes found medicinal uses for *Pinus strobus*. The Iroquois boiled it and inhaled the steam for relief from chest congestion. At either end of the white pine's range, the Menominee and the Micmac also used it for the common cold, and the Mohegans and the Montagnais and the Shinnecock each chewed pine pitch as natural cough drops.

Wounds were treated with pine poultices by many tribes. The Chippewa used a concoction made from the pine to stave off infection and gangrene, and the Delaware placed poultices on sores to draw out poisons and to relieve boils. The Iroquois and the Menominee did the same with splinters and thorns. The Micmac stopped hemorrhages by filling lacerations with pine sap. The Potawatomi made a salve out of crushed pine bark and wood. The Ojibwa boiled up mashed pine needles and used the steam for headaches and backaches. The Delaware made rubs for babies and ingested ground twigs for kidney and heart ailments. The Iroquois treated stomach pain and cramps the same way.

When it was time to lie down at night, the Ojibwa crawled onto beds of pine boughs. Piled on the floor of a wigwam and covered with blankets, freshly cut branches lifted sleepers off the ground, providing an insulating layer and removing them from any moisture, and they filled the sleeping space with their beautiful fragrance.

Many tribes used the lumber of pine trees to make canoes, shelters, and simply as firewood. And many also put boiled pitch to work as a caulk for weatherproofing boats, ideas that the Europeans would borrow from them.

The pine's usefulness was not confined to the material world, either. Burning needles were believed to ward off evil as well as sickness. In the spring and fall Iroquois tribes would burn needles to fill their longhouses with smoke, ridding their living space of any disease or unwanted spirits. Flaming branches would also be waved at individuals suspected of being possessed by ghosts or dark forces as a form of exorcism.

In many ways, the eastern white pine proved worthy of the faith the natives vested it with. It gave of itself endlessly, keeping them alive in winter, curing their ailments, ridding their houses of evil spirits. And of course, it brought peace, according to legend. In a ceremony in 1987—three hundred years after the French Marquis de Denonville and his native allies wiped out Ganondagan to punish the Seneca for trading with the English—Peter Jemison and other tribal leaders founded Ganondagan State Historic Site in Victor, New York. Southeast of Rochester, the site was home to the largest Seneca village in history, and there were concerns that the sacred land might be developed. An Iroquois advisory committee formed and together saved Ganondagan, creating a park and visitor center. Guests can walk miles of trails and tour a full-size replica of a seventeenth-century longhouse, and they can walk the Earth Is Our Mother trail to find a ceremonial white pine "Tree of Peace" planted at the founding of Ganondagan to honor the community's Iroquois roots. Every June, native Iroquois gather at the site for a Thanksgiving prayer during National Sacred Places Prayer Days, celebrating the Peacemaker, the union they founded so many years ago, and the tree that showed them the way.

CHAPTER TWO

The Forest for the Trees

It was the white pine that of all the timber resources of the North American continent first attracted the attention of explorers.

—J. E. DEFEBAUGH

ON THE EIGHTEENTH OF MAY, 1605, THEY FINALLY MADE landfall. Captain George Weymouth and his crew of twenty-nine had been sailing for two months in search of the fabled country called Virginia. They had shoved off from England aboard the *Archangel* on Easter and had been forced by steady, prevailing winds to take a more northerly course than they had wanted. After almost eight weeks of travel they still had not seen the misty shores of the New World.

Captain Weymouth, an experienced sailor and mathematician from Devon, knew these waters better than most—he'd voyaged to North America three years prior, looking for the Northwest Passage to India on behalf of the Dutch East India Company. This time he was sailing at the behest of English merchants, but his goal was quite different—the colonization of Virginia. The crew knew the helm was gripped by the hands of a veteran. One of the men aboard the ship, James Rosier, employed to document the adventure, said Weymouth knew "most of the Coast of

England and most of other Countries (having beene experienced by imployments in discoveries and travails from his childehood)."[1]

Even so, Rosier and others aboard began to worry by the middle of May. Weymouth may have known what he was doing, but the Atlantic was temperamental and unpredictable. The *Archangel* had had generally fair travels, but they'd encountered a few difficulties as they approached North America, and doubts began to rise like the tide. The ship entered areas of rock and shoal, which looked ideal for perforating the hull, and the men aboard found their eyes fooled by tricks of the sea, spotting cliffs that turned out to be clouds. On May 16 their navigator consulted his maps and sailed directly toward the shore—only to find that the continent drawn on the chart had completely disappeared.

"We stood in directly with the land," wrote Rosier, "and much marvelled we descried it not, wherein we found our sea charts very false, putting land where none is."[2]

And there were those among the crew who knew that, while Weymouth had sailed these shores before, things had not always gone well. On the captain's 1602 journey, his ship *Discovery* encountered dangerous fog and floating ice that almost overturned their small craft, and they battled a violent August storm—it got so bad several of the thirty-five crewmen mutinied, taking control of the ship. Weymouth returned to England in defeat.

This spring would prove to be different. Just two days after the phantom coast episode, all was well. On a fine May day, the *Archangel* reached a tall island where they fished for "thirty great cods and hadocks," refilled their water casks, and anchored beneath tall cliffs for the night. When they shoved off in the morning, they saw the "maine," unmistakable this time for its "high mountains." They coasted in among more small islands and found a sheltered place to drop anchor.[3]

The crew was relieved to have reached the New World, wrote Rosier. "We all with great joy praised God for his unspeakable goodnesse, who had from so apparent danger delivered us, &

directed us upon this day into so secure an Harbour: in remembrance whereof we named it Pentecost harbor."[4]

They spent the next days exploring from their new berth, finding evidence on one island that someone had been there before them—a fire ring and "the bones of some beast."[5] But they saw nothing and nobody in the dense woods—except trees. And they were astonished at the forest they found themselves in.

All around them and as far as the eye could see, trees raked the sky. To Weymouth and his crew these woodlands represented one thing—naval stores. Their native land was almost devoid of any trees useful for shipbuilding—those had been cut long ago. Here oaks for hulls and pine for masts numbered in the tens of thousands—and that was hard by the sea. The forest seemed to stretch on forever inland.

And the British Isles had nothing of the sort. The English had become dependent upon masts from Norway and the Baltics to an almost desperate degree. The sea was the very lifeblood of the kingdom's commerce, and much of England's military might came from its navy. To build the empire they desired, to keep up with the French and the Spanish and the Dutch, to grow and prosper as a nation, to outfit a strong armada, the British needed a steady supply of masts.

British ships of the line would have a mainmast more than three feet in diameter at its base, and for every inch of width, the spar was a yard tall. Which meant, of course, to fit a tall ship with a new mast, a fairly massive tree was needed. The bole had to be tall and straight, free of rot—and at least 108 feet.

Lacking the necessary timber on their own shores, they had turned to the forests of Russia and Bosnia and Norway to supply them. There, they found *Pinus sylvestris*, Scotch fir, which, while far from ideal, was adequate for the job. However, few of the firs that the English bought from the Baltics were bigger than twenty-seven inches, and no single tree could reach the heights needed, so masts were typically cobbled together. Multiple sections were laid end on end and bound at the joints with wide bands of iron. This worked, but it amounted to a mast that was already compromised and never as strong as one from single tree would be.

"Within the llands growe wood of sundry sorts, some very great, and all tall," wrote Rosier.

Birch, Beech, Ash, Maple, Spruce, Cherry-tree, Yew, Oke very great and good, Firre-tree, out of which issueth Turpentine in so marvellous plenty, and so sweet, as our chirurgeon and others affirmed they never saw so good in England. We pulled off much Gumme congealed on the outside of the barke, which smelted like Frankincense. This would be a great benefit for making Tarre and Pitch.[6]

They were ideal for naval stores. The resins of the white pine, as the natives knew, made exceptional caulk, for waterproofing hulls. And their timber was excellent for masts. Plenty tall and wide enough, a single tree could stand for a spar, and, because of the natural elasticity of its wood and the long life of its resins, the pine would sway in a wind and not break. They were relatively light, with an exceptional strength-to-weight ratio, and they were easy to work, and resilient.

Wherever Weymouth and his company went along what is now the midcoast of Maine, they continued to marvel at the forests. "And surely it did all resemble a stately Parke," wrote Rosier, "wherein appeare some old trees with high withered tops, and other flourishing with living greene boughs. Upon the hilles grow notable high timber trees, masts for ships of 400 tun."[7]

Weymouth had been hired by wealthy Englishmen—in this case Thomas Arundell, the Baron of Wardour, and Henry Wriothesley, the third Earl of Southampton—to explore Virginia and report back on "the commodities and profits of the countrey, together with the fitnesse of plantation."[8] Weymouth would do the exploring; James Rosier, the reporting.

The crew's first two tasks were jobs that would forever be linked with the coast where they landed—cutting trees and shipbuilding. Weymouth's crew set about felling pines to repair their ship and constructing a shallop, a small sailboat for coastal cruising, which they had brought in pieces aboard the *Archangel*. "We cut yards, waste trees, and many necessaries for our ship, while our Carpenter and Cooper laboured to fit and furnish forth the shallop."[9] Work began under the supervision of their indefatigable leader, whose "labour was ever as much or rather more than any mans," as Rosier put it.

George Weymouth and James Rosier weren't the first Europeans—or even the first Englishmen—to be overwhelmed by the plenty of the New World, especially where the woodlands were concerned. Perhaps the first to mention the forest for the trees was the Portuguese explorer Gaspar Cortereal, who visited Newfoundland or Labrador in 1501 and instantly recognized the potential sprouting from the ground in front of him. He described what he found to his king: "They have also great store of wood and above all of pines for making masts and yards of ships."[10] Despite Cortereal's glowing report, the Portuguese concentrated their empire-building efforts elsewhere.

Two decades later came the Italian Giovanni Verrazano. The term *Acadia*, which would become standard for Europeans to describe the northeast of North America—especially what's now Maine, New Brunswick, and Nova Scotia—came from Verrazano's account of a trip sailing along the coast north of Virginia in 1524 looking for passage to the Orient. The Italian sailor called this new world "Arcadia," referring to the Edenic land of unspoiled wilderness of Greek poetry, "on account of the beauty of the trees." Like Cortereal, he wrote breathlessly to his king: "Nearby we could see a stretch of country much higher than the sandy shore, with many beautiful fields and plains full of great forests, some sparse and some dense; and the trees have so many colors, and are so beautiful and delightful that they defy description."[11]

And, of course, standing above those many hued trees were stately eastern white pines. "Keeping more to the north, we found high country full of very dense forests, composed of pines, cypresses, and similar trees which grow in cold regions."[12]

A year after Verrazano, Portuguese explorer Esteban Gomez crossed the Atlantic, making landfall at Newfoundland in 1525. He was put on the tail of the Italian explorer by Charles V of Spain, who had learned of Verrazano's journey and wanted to beat his rivals to the riches of Asia. Piloting *La Anunciada*, Gomez arrived in February and cruised up the St. Lawrence River, spending a cold winter along the wide waterway. In the spring, he threaded his way down the Bay of Fundy along what's now the coast of Maine, sailing up the Penobscot River and then cruising south at least as far as Newport, Rhode Island, but possibly to New Jersey. Gomez was impressed with the "temperate, well-forested"[13] landscape, but he never did find the passage to India or the gold Charles V wanted. And the Spanish abandoned the northeast, concentrating their explorations to the southeast and southwest.

All this talk of riches and resources caught the attention of the English. First and foremost they didn't want to get left in the wake of their rivals. They too wanted passage to Asia, and they were also intrigued by the idea of precious metals, figuring Gomez must have simply overlooked them. You couldn't set foot in the New World without tripping over a gold nugget—at least that was what many British speculators thought—and the early charters of English sailors contained language that reserved a percentage of such findings for the crown.

It didn't take the English long, however, to figure out what was truly valuable to them in North America—money genuinely did grow on trees. As early as 1583 merchants like Christopher Carliell were arguing that England ought to look to America for its resources, using it as a sort of bargain warehouse, colonizing the continent as a means to secure and ready timber and tar and pitch and fish for shipment back to the mother country. He wrote to the

Muscovy Company in 1583 to convince them to turn away from the Baltics and toward America for naval stores. If they built a foothold in the New World, he maintained, England could acquire fish, furs, masts, and tar, "without being in any sort beholding to a king of Denmarke, or other prince or state that shall be in such sort able to command our shippes at their pleasure, as those doe at this day, by meanes of their strait passages and strong shipping."[14]

And Captain Carliell wasn't alone. That same year, Sir George Peckham, an English venture capitalist, added his voice to the colonization chorus, arguing that America could be something of a natural resource supermart, supplying England with furs, silk, fruits, metals, jewels, hemp, feathers, and, of course, the pines for masts necessary to maintain their status as a world power. Peckham was adamant it was time for his countrymen to wake "out of that drowsy dream wherein we have so long slumbered."[15]

Colonization for the purpose of trade was, in fact, why George Weymouth and his crew were picking their way along "the maine" in search of Virginia. Captain Weymouth's remit was very similar to that of Bartholomew Gosnold, who had explored what is now the coast of Maine three years prior, sponsored by several of the same investors behind Weymouth's voyage.

Gosnold even brought along twenty people "to remain in the country for population."[16] Weymouth's scribe James Rosier also sailed with him, along with another reporter, who wrote of a land "full of fair trees"[17] and later mentioned "trees tall and straight."[18] A year later, in 1603, Martin Pring crossed the Atlantic in the *Speedwell* to explore the possibilities of settling northern Virginia. Pring had violent run-ins with natives—they tried to set his ship afire—but still came back fairly glowing about all that he'd seen.

"Howbeit we beheld very goodly Groves and Woods replenished with tall Okes, Beeches, Pinetrees, Firre-trees, Hasels, Wichhasels, and Maples. We saw here also sundry sorts of Beasts, as Stags, Deere, Beares, Wolves, Foxes, Lusernes, and Dogges with sharpe noses."[19]

Weymouth and his crew spent about a month gunkholing along the coast of what is now New England, having countless adventures with the natives. Weymouth dazzled them by magnetizing his sword and magically using it to pick up metal objects. He also tempted them with snap peas, which they loved and had never seen, and lured them aboard the *Archangel*, only to kidnap them, like a playground snatcher with candy. Two paddled out to see the ship and were enticed on board and stuffed into a hold. Three others were physically taken, grabbed by the top knot, and hauled across the decks.

When they finally turned for home on June 16, Weymouth and crew had aboard five Abenaki natives captured to show to the king and his sponsors. They were specimens, forced to explain their culture, governance, and homeland to give the English a thorough understanding of this place they planned to conquer.

Also in the hold were various other items collected from the New World. And among them were several samples of *Pinus strobus*, the eastern white pine, the perfect tree for masting ships.

CHAPTER THREE

Trees across the Seas

The woodman in the forest hews, the kingly mast to rear,
And forth the fearless vessel goes to earth's remotest sphere;
But who of all the mariners upon the watery plain
Gives praise to that unswerving knight, who loved the hills
*   of Maine?*

—L. H. SIGOURNEY, HARTFORD,
CONNECTICUT, NOVEMBER 5, 1862[1]

WHEN THE *ARCHANGEL* DOCKED AT PLYMOUTH, ENGLAND, IN 1606, Sir Ferdinando Gorges was there to meet Captain George Weymouth and to hear an account of his voyage. The forty-year-old Englishman was one of the sponsors of the trip, though not as heavily invested as were the Baron of Wardour or the Earl of Southampton. Gorges was overjoyed to see Weymouth—the knight had an almost childlike glee about anything where the New World was concerned. Growing up in Clerkenwell, Middlesex, he had been intrigued by the epic adventures of Francis Drake, John Hawkins, and the Gilbert brothers, all of them mariners who sailed over far horizons and fought for Queen Elizabeth I against the notorious Spanish Armada. Not only did those men go where no other Europeans had, but several of them talked of settling those strange lands in the New World. Sir Humphrey Gilbert was among the first granted a royal charter "for planting our people in America,"[2] as early as June of 1578. A far-off wilderness world, battles against superpowers, an empire for England—it was heady stuff for a young boy.

By the time he was in his twenties, Gorges was adventuring overseas like his heroes. He too went to war against the fabled Spanish Armada and fought in the French Wars of Religion. During those conflicts, he and other English Protestants lent their swords to the Huguenots against the Catholics in what was largely a French civil war. Gorges had a distinguished, eventful campaign—promoted to captain at the Siege of Sluys in 1587, taken prisoner in 1587, exchanged for prisoners of the Armada and cited for bravery, wounded at the Siege of Paris in 1589—before being knighted by the Second Earl of Essex in 1591 at the Siege of Rouen. Upon his return home, he was promoted to the position of governor of the Fort at Plymouth, which was where Weymouth found him.

Disembarking in England with Weymouth and Rosier were the five natives who Weymouth's crew had kidnapped in New England. Gorges took three of them into his custody. During the crossing, Weymouth had taught the captives enough English to allow them to carry on rudimentary conversations, and Gorges eagerly brought them to his home, where he began to pump them for information. Gorges spent hours talking with the Americans, getting a picture of their home country, and he loved what he heard. A friend of Sir Walter Raleigh, one of England's most famous and ardent proponents of colonization, the young knight was already fully behind the idea of expanding Britain's empire in America, and, thanks to the bits and pieces he was able to gather from his captured confidantes, he became even more obsessed.

"The longer I conversed with them," he wrote,

the better hope they gave me of those parts where they did inhabit, as proper for our uses; especially when I found what

goodly rivers, stately islands and safe harbors those parts
abounded with. . . . And having kept them full three years, I
made them able to set me down what great rivers ran up into
the land, what men of note were seated on them, what power
they were of, how allied, what enemies they had and the like.[3]

For Gorges, the moment he met the native trio was a turning
point in history. "This accident must be acknowledged the means
under God," he wrote, "of putting on foot and giving life to all
our plantations."[4] In other words, the governor's acquaintance
with these three Abenakis helped birth the English colonization
of North America.

The enthusiastic knight began to make alliances with men—
of means—equally keen on planting English seeds in the New
World. Several influential Englishmen, including Gorges's good
friend, the much older Sir Walter Raleigh, had spent the previous
few decades trying to drum up interest in exploiting the resources
of North America. In 1574 a handful of them, including Sir
Humphrey Gilbert, Sir George Peckham, and Sir Richard Gren-
ville, petitioned the queen for the right to explore and discover
land in North America "fatally reserved for England, and for the
honor of your majesty."[5] And Raleigh claimed a patent for a colony in Virginia dating back to 1584.

Like businessmen everywhere, these early imperialists were
interested in this new continent for those eternal reasons: money
and power. Not only did the New World have much of what the
British Isles lacked—namely timber, precious metals, furs, and
even sassafras—their rivals the Spanish were already reaping the
benefits of their explorations and colonial efforts. The Iberians were
shipping home a fortune in gold and silver from *their* colonies, and
the English didn't want to lose ground. Spain's interests were in the
southeast and southwest of the sprawling continent, but no nation
had built successful colonies in the northeast, though France had
tried. The English, too, had attempted it—sending settlers over

to start the "Lost Colony" of Roanoke in 1585. Many, including Gorges, felt they had to up their efforts and make another go.

England had several simple reasons for wanting to build a haven in North America. It would show the world England's power—nations with more territory were obviously bigger and grander, and thus more important. During this time of growing religious conflict, they could expand the word of God, setting up a new region full of English speakers who worshipped as they did. English vessels could harass the Spanish and retreat to safe North American harbors from the battles with Spain, holing up, making repairs, and taking on supplies. Further, Great Britain was relatively small, and even in the late sixteenth century many of the wealthy were finding it crowded and disliked being forced into proximity with undesirables. Setting up a plantation would allow England to move some of its population—especially the poor and indigent—elsewhere. And while those unfortunate Englishmen were in North America they could busy themselves by procuring supplies for the mother country. It was perfect.

As early as 1584, Richard Hakluyt, a writer and geographer, was arguing for just such a system of colonies in the New World. That year, his book *Discourse on Western Planting* made what was likely the first published case for colonization. Hakluyt was steeped in the stuff early—he was raised by a cousin, a lawyer and businessman, after the death of his father, and grew up in a household visited by some of the most prominent investors, explorers, and cartographers of the time. After stints at Westminster School and Christ Church, Oxford, he was ordained and took a job as a professor of geography at Oxford.

Not only did Hakluyt believe the English should build plantations in America, he thought they should do so specifically because of the pines—or rather the woodland resources. He envisioned a system where settlers would erect sawmills on waterways and fell trees that could be then shipped back to England. Coopers could find the oak for their barrel staves, more oaks could be dropped for ships' hulls, bark by-products could be collected for the tanning industry, and the soaring pines could be harvested for ship's masts.

Hakluyt continued his case in *The Principal Navigations, Voyages, Traffiques and Discoveries of the English Nation*, published five years after *Discourse on Western Planting*. Long a student of the travels and findings of European explorers—especially where North America was concerned—the geographer had an extensive library of maps, charts, and memoirs documenting the overseas adventures of the likes of Gosnold and Pring and Gilbert. And he included his collection in his 1589 work, enumerating the many benefits England could derive from the continent. "This realm shall receive . . . most or all the commodities that we receive from the best parts of Europe, and we shall receive the same better cheap than now we receive them." Among these resources he noted were furs, fish, marble, and forest products. "Since great waste woods be there of oak, cedar, pine, walnuts, and sundry other sorts, many of our waste people may be employed in making of ships, hoys, busses, and boats, and in making of rosin, pitch, and tar."[6]

Many agreed with Hakluyt, though some did not. Arguments for and against colonization filled taverns and legal chambers. An anonymous paper was published making the case that the government should officially aid and sponsor the settlement of America for the same reasons Hakluyt had posited—to secure a steady supply of naval stores—especially pine trees for masts. The Kingdom of England was wholly dependent upon the seas for both its commerce and national security, the argument went, which required ships and the ability to build and fit out ships. The country could not produce masts or turpentine on her own and could secure them "only by the favor of forraigne potency."[7]

Sir Ferdinando Gorges certainly agreed. He argued in a state paper in 1600 that it would behoove England to turn its attention to North America because this "newfound land" had the "commodities necessary for shipping," and "necessities to ower navye . . . there in abundance."[8]

But to mount a successful English colony in North America, Gorges, Hakyluyt, and their allies needed the backing of the crown.

Soon after Weymouth and the *Archangel* returned to England, James Rosier published his account of the voyage. Titled *A True Relation of the most prosperous voyage made this present year by Captaine George Waymouth in the Discovery of the Land of Virginia: where he discovered 60 miles of a most excellent River; together with a most fertile land* (London, 1605), Rosier's memoir brims with enthusiasm for the place. Its depiction of the continent, its people, and its resources only broadened the interest in America already growing in England. He and Weymouth had crossed the seas as a sort of feasibility study of North America as a potential English colony, and they found the wild continent couldn't be more suited to their plans. Rosier's work inspired hundreds of individuals in high places in British government, among them Sir John Popham. The lord chief justice of England, Popham was born in 1531 to a family of knights. He went to Balliol College, Oxford, and studied the classics and divinity before becoming a justice of the peace. He became a Member of Parliament, rose to speaker of the House of Commons at age fifty, and later that year became the nation's attorney general. He was about as eminent an ally as Gorges could have wanted. The pair had a history—when Popham was arrested and imprisoned while working for Mary, Queen of Scots, he was broken out and ferried to safety by his old friend.

Popham had taken in the other two natives from North America captured and carried across the ocean by Weymouth, and like Gorges, he was keenly impressed by their tales of their home. Rosier's glowing descriptions in his book were simply more confirmation bias. Sir Popham became convinced that North America held the key to maintaining English greatness, and he and Gorges began to draw up plans for a colonization attempt. With his high rank and legal background, Justice John Popham was perfectly placed to get the royal approval such a project would need.

It didn't take long.

On April 10, 1606, King James I gave his royal nod, issuing a charter to Gorges, Popham, Richard Hakluyt, Raleigh Gilbert, William Parker, Sir Thomas Gates, and Sir George Somers, among others, "for the planting of colonies or plantations in North America."[9] The king granted these nobles permission to settle between the 34th and 45th parallels, or, roughly, between what's now South Carolina and Maine. Two corporations were founded for this purpose, one to settle South Virginia and the other to settle North Virginia. The London Company would sow seeds in the south, between the 34th and 41st parallels. The Plymouth Company would plant itself in the north, between the 41st and 45th parallels. When they were established and healthy, the stronger colony would be allowed to expand into the overlapping territory.

Gorges and Popham wasted little time, sending out their first vessel, piloted by a Captain Haines, within a month, "to settle a plantation in the river of Sagadahoc,"[10] in the area where George Weymouth had visited. Haines sailed in May 1606 but was quickly intercepted by the Spanish, and the venture died with him. In high summer, they tried again, this time with a ship captained by Henry Challong. It, too, was captured by the Spanish. Martin Pring, who had explored the coast of North America in 1603, ventured across the Atlantic in October, looking for Challong. Unable to find the captain, he cruised the shore, looking for the best places to put down roots. When Pring made it back to England he met with Gorges and Popham, and they decided to make a full-scale effort in Sagadahoc, the name they gave for the general area where Weymouth landed. They would send everything needed for a colony in the next year.

In May 1607, two ships sailed from Plymouth for what is now the Maine coast. Sir John Popham's nephew, George, was at the helm of the *Gift of God*, with Raleigh Gilbert as his second in command. Gilbert was the son of Gorges's friend Sir Humphrey

Gilbert and a relation of Sir Walter Raleigh. The other ship, *Mary and John*, was piloted by Robert Davies. Between the two, the vessels carried more than a hundred settlers, among them fifteen "gentlemen," members of the English gentry, along with tradesmen, artisans, soldiers, and all the tools and supplies needed to construct a new town on a far shore.

This time they made it. Barely.

The *Gift of God* reached the mouth of the Kennebec River—the same area where Weymouth had nosed about in 1606; a cross he erected was still there—on August 13, 1607, and the *Mary and John* cruised in three days later.[11] Gilbert's ship had been delayed when he was detained by Flemish sailors, and several aboard were imprisoned. The *Gift of God* didn't see her distress signals and had continued on.

But here they all were, finally. It was a beautiful stretch of coastline, characterized by sandy beaches and tall pines. Gilbert and Popham went upriver in search of a suitable place to build their town, and Gilbert was impressed by the islands he saw "all rockye and full of pine trees."[12] Atop a bosky headland, overlooking a small cove, they found a site they deemed suitable, and the colonists began to construct a star-shaped bastion they named Fort St. George, hoping England's patron saint would bring their new venture some luck.

They built a serious compound, erecting a storehouse, chapel, and dwellings—more than a dozen buildings in total. And in early fall, they sent the *Mary and John* to England for more supplies.

Back in Plymouth, Sir Ferdinando Gorges was excited to learn of the developments at Sagadahoc. He took the tidings from the supply ship to the Earl of Salisbury, who was a member of the Privy Council, a group of advisors to the king, telling him the intrepid English settlers had met with "gallant rivers, stately harbors, and a people tractable." He hailed reports of an abundance of fish and fine timber, writing that "the certainty of the commodities that may be had from so fertile a soil as that is, when it shall be peopled, as well for building of shipping, having all things rising in the place wherewith to do it."[13]

But he was bothered by reports of the difficulties some settlers were having in the new land and rumblings about abandoning the venture. Many found the landscape inhospitable, and there was infighting and politicking as cliques formed around Popham and the younger Raleigh Gilbert. As winter approached, about half of the new colonists decided this New World wilderness was not for them. They didn't like the frigid winds that buffeted their headland, and they had trouble procuring food, since they arrived in late summer and had no time to plant crops. In December, the disaffected settlers returned to the comforts of England aboard the *Gift of God*.

Neither Raleigh Gilbert nor George Popham were among them. Popham especially liked what he saw of Sagadahoc, and it only solidified in his mind the rightness of his mission. He sent a letter aboard the *Gift of God* addressed to King James: "My well considered opinion is, that in these regions the glory of God may be easily evidenced, the empire of your Majesty enlarged and the welfare of the Britons speedily augmented."[14]

The forty-five settlers who remained in the Popham colony hunkered down, bracing themselves for the trying winter to come. They were amazed to see the Kennebec River freeze over. Hardship followed on hardship. One of their storehouses burned. They were not initially successful in their efforts to befriend the natives. And at least one colonist died, not nearly as many as their counterparts lost down in warmer Jamestown.

But the settler who passed away was an integral one. George Popham died on February 5, 1608, at the age of fifty-eight. Raleigh Gilbert became president of the venture. A supply ship brought word that one of the colony's major sponsors, Sir John Popham (George's uncle), had died in England, and that Raleigh Gilbert had inherited a castle in Devon. Suddenly, Sagadahoc's young leader wanted to go home. At a single turn, the Popham colony lost one of their primary backers and their captain in the field. The settlement couldn't survive these losses, and the remaining forty-five colonists decided to join Gilbert on his return.

The Popham colony was not a complete failure, however, and it very quietly made its mark on history. Happy to have made it through the bitter winter, the settlers of Fort George celebrated what many historians consider to be the first Thanksgiving in North America, predating the Pilgrims by thirteen years. The lessons they learned were very helpful in the planning of the Plymouth colony that would follow them in Massachusetts Bay, and they made England's first claim to *New* England.

They also proved something that would be pivotal to the growth of the region. One of the missions of the colony was to test Richard Hakluyt's theory that North America would make for a fine place to build ships. It had everything they needed— massive oaks for hulls, soaring pines for masts, and resins for caulking. The Popham colonists hammered this idea into material form, building the first ship by Europeans in North America, a thirty-ton pinnace they named *Virginia*. In August, it was aboard that ship that they returned to the fair shores of Great Britain, making it almost exactly a year in the New World.

The 104 settlers in South Virginia fared better in some ways, worse in others. One of the first things mentioned when their three ships approached land was the soaring tree cover they spied. "Wee descried the Land of Virginia," wrote scribe George Percy, "there wee landed and discovered a liitle way, but wee could find nothing worth the spending of, but faire meadows and goodly tall trees."[15]

In the months after their homes were built and the settlement was secure, Captain John Smith (of Pocahontas fame) spent time exploring. The famous adventurer was struck by what he saw around him. He described the hills and dunes, and the "great plentie of Pines and Firres." The Virginia coastline was "all overgrowne with Trees and weeds, being a plaine Wilderness as God first made it."[16] He was impressed with the "odoriferous Gumme"[17] he found on some evergreens, which made it ideal for caulking hulls, and found the region fairly idyllic.

"The mildnesse of the aire the fertilitie of the soile, and the situation of the Rivers, are so propitious to the nature and use of man, as no place is more convenient for pleasure, profit, and man's sustenance."[18]

Smith and his fellow colonists named the village they constructed Jamestown after their king, and even though they lost more than 135 of their number to malaria, fever, and dysentery, they eventually prospered.

Perhaps no one watched for news from the new plantations with more eagerness than Sir Ferdinando Gorges. He was deeply troubled when he heard that the Popham colony had disbanded. "All our former hopes were frozen to death,"[19] he wrote later. He would rally, and look for positives. England couldn't give up on colonization. It was too important. The benefits were too many—"the boldness of the coast, the easiness of the navigation, the fertility of the soil, and the several sorts of commodities that they are assured the country do yield, as namely fish in the season in great plenty."[20]

And, he wrote, "all along the coast mastidge for ships."[21]

Gorges's unending enthusiasm for English plantations would set him in good stead—though he never made it to North America himself, never once explored the woods that his native friends had him dreaming about. In August 1622, two years after the Pilgrims arrived in the *Mayflower* and set permanent English roots in New England, the Plymouth Council for New England, a spinoff of the Plymouth Company, granted Sir Ferdinando Gorges and John Mason a land patent for territory that would become the provinces of New Hampshire of Maine. All the land between the Merrimac and Kennebec rivers, a vast region stretching two hundred miles, through the finest white pine country the colonists had found, was now his.

CHAPTER FOUR

The Dominion of New England

The pine stays green in winter . . . wisdom in hardship.
—NORMAN DOUGLAS

AS THE SUN CAME UP ON APRIL 18, 1689, A LARGE GROUP OF angry Bostonians—provincial militia and Puritan leaders alike—began to gather in the growing communities of Charlestown and Roxbury. Those in the former rowed across the Charles River; those in the latter marched into the city. Edward Randolph knew full well what was about to happen. He'd been in the colonies long enough, working as a royal customs agent and surveyor of the woods, to see where things were going.

When the news from England first reached Boston, his colleague Edmund Andros, the governor of the New England colonies, immediately moved to have the messengers arrested. Both men could see, just as rabble follows ale, what would occur when this mob discovered that King James II had been deposed by William of Orange and his English allies.

The city had already begun to boil, filled with Puritans suspicious of the work Randolph and Andros were doing for the king, furious that a monarch far across the sea would dare to revoke the charter of Massachusetts Bay. Since the first plantation took root in Virginia and Massachusetts, the English population of the

New World had ballooned. More than 150,000 had migrated to the colonies—Massachusetts alone had upwards of 40,000 residents—and it didn't take them long to get their own ideas about how life should be in their new home. Within a decade of landing, the Puritans who founded the city organized the first Massachusetts General Court and started issuing laws. They quickly began to try the patience of King Charles II, and he returned the favor.

The crown decided it needed to rein in these colonial upstarts and instituted the Navigational Acts, beginning in 1651, placing restrictions on trade. It enacted new duties on commerce in 1673, and sued Massachusetts Bay colony for trade violations in 1678. In 1684, King Charles II annulled the charter of Massachusetts, placing the colony under royal commission. Residents of New England were incensed, especially those in Boston. They were angered further when he folded their province into the Dominion of New England, a new entity created for the express purpose of limiting colonial autonomy. Into these mean streets the king inserted first Randolph and later Andros to exercise authority.

Both men were sure that, if the colonists heard that King James had been deposed, they would revolt themselves. Andros wrote to an officer of the militia at Pemaquid, a Maine outpost surrounded by mast pines, about a "general buzzing among the people, great with expectation of their old charter."[1] The news of England's Glorious Revolution couldn't be contained, and Randolph and Andros knew it wouldn't be long before a posse formed on the streets of the capital and came looking for them.

They were right.

The mob that moved into the city at dawn took the captain of the British gunship HMS *Rose* into custody first, and later arrested Edward Randolph. The Puritans hauled off numerous English officials in turn, locking them in the Boston Gaol, an ugly place on Prison Street with stone walls thirty-six inches thick and doors bristling with iron spikes. A visitor described the passageways between its cells "like the dark valley of the shadow of death."[2]

Governor Andros attempted to make a hasty getaway. He thought he would find safety aboard the HMS *Rose*, not knowing that the mob had been there first. When he found that wouldn't save him, he eventually gave up. The men of Massachusetts told him that they "must and would have the Government in their own hands."[3]

The Puritans called the uprising their own Glorious Revolution, and they assumed governance of the Massachusetts Bay colony. A similar scene played out in New York, where wealthy fur trader Jacob Leisler and a band of rebels led their own little coup against Andros's underling, Lieutenant Governor Francis Nicholson, and seized control of the city.

Edward Randolph sat in prison and seethed. It wasn't the first time he'd been arrested. Ten years earlier, just about to make a trip to America to continue to hunt for violations of the Navigation Acts, he was detained in his own country, right near the Royal Exchange of London. Some of his enemies had used one of Randolph's debts to trump up charges against him. He was able to clear his name quickly but it taught it him to watch his back more closely. He was arrested numerous times in Boston as well while trying to enforce the king's trade laws—local businessmen used it as a tool to harass English officials, cast doubt on their authority, and attempt to, as Randolph put it, "force me out of this Towne."[4]

The native of Canterbury had a lot of enemies—or, at least, it seemed a lot of people disliked him—and he had few friends even among his fellow English authorities. Randolph's prickly personality managed to turn many against him. When he was recommended to the Lord Treasurer for a position as a customs agent, the Commissioners of Customs referred to him as being "obnoxious to the hatred of the people,"[5] but they decided that shouldn't keep someone out of office and instated him anyway.

Others called him a "martinet,"[6] and those being generous claimed he was monomaniacal. But he was liked well enough in the highest quarters of England to earn his customs position and a side job—as surveyor of the woods for Massachusetts, Connecticut, and New Hampshire. In that position he was referred to as the "Evil Genius of New England" and "her Angel of death."[7]

His selection as surveyor of the woods was logical enough—he'd spent years working in naval stores. Randolph began by selling oaks from his own property in Kent to the Royal Navy, and in the 1660s he became a timber agent for the English government. He was so likeable in that capacity he ended up getting moved to the highlands of Scotland, to scout for trees far from England, and became embroiled in controversy there. His wife's cousin was Robert Mason, who owned a grant to forest lands in New Hampshire in the new colonies that he'd inherited from his father. After John Mason and Sir Ferdinando Gorges were given a patent to the lands between the Merrimac and Kennebec rivers, the pair divvied them up, with Mason keeping the territory south of the Piscataqua River—essentially New Hampshire—while Gorges took the deed to the north—essentially Maine. Mason described the woods of New Hampshire to Edward Randolph, and Randolph saw in them a New World, with new trees, and new opportunities—and a chance to leave his problems in England behind.

Because he was the face of the king, the unsmiling wig enforcing the crown's policies on shipping and trade, Randolph was unpopular immediately upon arriving in March 1676. Increase Mather, perhaps the most famous resident of New England at the time, called him "a mortal enemy to our country" and wrote that it was "good that all mankind should be convinced that he is a knave."[8]

Angering the Puritan locals went with the territory. Led by Increase and his son, Cotton Mather, the men of Boston objected to the way British authorities threw their weight around in the colony. The Mathers were particularly bothered that the crown wanted them to submit to the Church of England, that they disregarded their right to representation in local government, and eventually revoked their charter. Others were just as offended that many of their grants to land, like their charter, had been overruled or revoked. Never mind that the royal agents were sniffing around in the woodlands, telling New Englanders what trees they could cut.

The Lords of Trade, the haughty nickname of the king's merchant-minded Privy councilors, first sent Edward Randolph to the colonies to look into the complaints of the heirs of Sir Ferdinando Gorges, who had inherited rights to lands in Maine. A grant to the New England Company in 1628, which eventually became a royal commission in the form of the Massachusetts Bay charter, overlapped territory with Gorges's—both claimed Maine. Randolph's first job was to find representatives from the Commonwealth to go argue their case in London. While he was in Boston, Randolph sent many letters across the sea about the countless violations—and violators—of the Navigation Acts.

Randolph was offended by the naked abuses he claimed he saw among Boston businessmen. Despite the prohibitions against trade with foreign nations, and the duties dictated by the Navigation Acts, the merchants of Massachusetts Bay were sending goods to whomever they wanted—and keeping the profits.

And there was a lot of money to be made. By the end of the seventeenth century, Boston had evolved into a growing mercantile power. In many ways, the city on Massachusetts Bay was just what men like Richard Hakluyt envisioned when setting out their grand plans for colonization half a century earlier. New England was shipping fish and furs in record numbers.

And masts, too. In 1609, the Jamestown colony sent the first pine boles, "fower score," to England for use as masts, and that same year, Henry Hudson stopped along the coast of Maine to fell a new foremast for his ship.[9] The English authorities made note of the quality and potential quantity. A Captain Will Perse wrote back from Virginia in 1629: "no better ship timber to be found in the world."[10] They would soon have more. In July 1634 another cargo of long, heavy, unwieldy masts—New England's first shipment—rode the waves to Britain aboard the *Hercules* of Dover.

Hakluyt's vision of commercial ships being built on American shores was soon realized, as well.

In 1629, the New England Company, an offshoot of the Plymouth Company, sent a handful of shipwrights to North America to begin building ships. Two years later in 1631 the *Blessing of the Bay* was finished in Malden, Massachusetts. Manufacturing vessels was cheaper and easier in the colonies—that's where the oak for hulls and pine for masts could be found. They'd then sail back to the mother country for sale. Without the expense of importing the raw material, ships could be turned out 30 percent cheaper in America than they were in England, and they would quickly become the most profitable manufactured export during the colonial era.[11]

As the shipwrights hammered, sawmills began to hum in North America. Where the first one was built is open to argument. Some say that a sawmill was installed in the coastal village of Agamentico, the old name of York, Maine, in 1623, just a few years after the *Mayflower* arrived. This was supposedly done at the behest of Sir Ferdinando Gorges, who had been advocating for plantations for just this reason. The famed knight wrote: "I sent over my son and my nephew, Captain William Gorges, who had been my lieutenant in the Fort of Plymouth, with some other craftsmen for the building of houses and the erecting of sawmills."[12]

Others claim that the first mill was on the Salmon Falls River above Portsmouth and was built in 1631, shortly after the grant for that territory was issued to Mason and Gorges. And still others say that the earliest sawmill was in the town of Berwick, Maine, beginning operations in that same year. Regardless, it seems clear that by the early 1630s, within a twenty-mile radius of

Portsmouth, there was at least one sawmill cleaving boards out of white pine trees. The technology was simple, patented about thirty years earlier by a clever Dutch inventor named Cornelis Corneliszoon van Uitgeest, who attached a rod called a pitman arm to a windmill, using air currents to drive a vertically mounted straight saw blade, which mimicked the motion of two men on either end of a whipsaw.[13] Where rivers and streams were available, a waterwheel served as the motor.

New England had plenty of moving water, and even more mills began to sprout on riverbanks. Mill owners were granted free land and exempted from taxes as long as they pledged to "keepe the mill going for the Towne use." With mast trees falling and lesser pines being used for boards, it didn't take long for the woodlands of New England to go from a fine colonial ponytail to a bald pate. The trees that had so attracted Gomez and Pring and Weymouth and Gorges began to slowly vanish, replaced by fields of stumps and later pastures. Settlers across the region were clearing vast acreage to promote agriculture, and something had to be done with all those trees. The economy of the colonies began to hum—or rather, whine—thanks to the pines.

The Brits took notice. In 1624, the adventurer, proto-environmentalist, and travel writer Thomas Morton built his own village north of Plymouth on the shore of Quincy Bay. Morton was a controversial figure, living among the natives, which put him at odds with the devout Pilgrims thirty miles to the south. He published a paean to the landscape around him called *New English Canaan* in 1637, and it was notable for including an entire section about the trees of the New World. Considered the first work of environmentalism in North America, it apprised the Privy Council of what they could expect to find in New England. Of *Pinus strobus* he wrote:

> *Pine: of this sorte there is infinite store in some parts of the*
> *Country. I have travelled 10 miles together where is little*

or no other wood growing. And of these may be made rosin, pitch and tarre, which are such usefull commodities that if wee had them not from other Countries in Amity with England, our Navigation would decline. Then how great the commodity of it will be to our Nation, to have it of our owne, let any man judge.[14]

The English Captain Thomas Wiggin, who paid a visit to the plantation at "the Massachusetts," "the largest, best, and most prospering in all that land," was likewise impressed with what he saw. "The country," he wrote, "well stored with timber, and will afford cordage, pitch, and tar. The English, numbering about 2,000, and generally most industrious, have done more in three years than others in seven times that space and at a tenth of the expense."[15]

Another anonymous observer was of much the same mind: "It was credibly informed to the [Privy] Council, that this country would, in time, be very beneficial to England for masts."[16] The next year, those New England masts began to arrive. The northern colonies packaged up their initial shipment. The Royal Navy was glad to have another source—but not particularly happy with the costs involved. Because of the unwieldy nature of hundred-foot masts that could weigh eighteen tons, they were expensive to ship—the English could still get them for four times less per shipping ton from their suppliers in the Baltics. And so they did. Despite the fact that they had a friendly depot overflowing with pine—for which Hakluyt and Gorges and Popham and so many others had been advocating—they preferred to deal with masts from the east.

The consequence, of course, was that New England timber cutters simply went looking for other places to market their wares. They shipped masts to England's late enemy Spain, they supplied Portugal, and they began to trade with the Canary Islands and Azores, the "wine islands," sending oak staves for barrels for their rosados and tintos. But they also sold a lot of lumber of the pino blanco variety. They made wide boards for sheathing homes and flooring and clapboards for siding. They made fat beams and posts for timber framing, and moulding for fancying up.

Pinus strobus began falling at an amazing rate—"Pines for masts the best in the world,"[17] as Edward Randolph put it—and the fragrant conifers were run down rivers to ports, shaped into masts, and loaded onto transports. They were also turned into other naval stores, like pine pitch for hulls.

Within 20 years, Boston would become the busiest port on the continent, and by the 1660s, the Iberian Peninsula had become the primary market for New England. Boston also shipped timber to Barbados in exchange for sugar and rum, and masts and other goods to the Dutch. By the turn of the eighteenth century, timber was making some New England merchants, "as rich as any man in England," and it built a very healthy merchant marine. "[The] Puritans controlled one of the strongest shipping trades outside of the Dutch Empire."[18]

England, the architect of this pine plantation system, wasn't happy.

The crown didn't like the independence these New Englanders were showing. The businessmen of Boston saw no reason to listen to a king from far away, and they ignored authorities like customs agent and surveyor of the woods Edward Randolph. They were quite pleased with their buyers in Spain and had no interest in discontinuing trade with New Netherlands just because England was at war with the Dutch. England's 1650s wars with the Dutch made masts all the more precious a commodity. They were needed not only to replace those spars being mowed down by cannon fire during the conflict's many sea battles but also to make up for those that were missing or delayed from the Baltic. Ruling the seas was crucial to the British—and they needed the tools to do it.

The Dutch were keenly aware of this, patrolling the sound and keeping vessels carrying naval stores from making it to England. One Dutch admiral, Maarten Harpertszoon Tromp, boasted that he had swept the English from the seas, and tied a broom handle to his masthead as a symbolic thumb of the nose. The shortage of spars that followed the Dutch blockade was painful, and something of an eye opener, and the English navy desperately turned back to New England for pines.

As William Carlton put it in a 1939 piece in the *New England Quarterly*: "It was not until the first Dutch War, in 1654, when the Dutch and Danes succeeded in cutting off her Eastland supply by closing 'the Sound,' the narrow strait which connects the North Sea with the Baltic, that Britain began to appreciate her colonial resources."[19]

And appreciate them they did. The Council of State, another spinoff of the Privy Council, asked the Governors and Commissioners of the United Colonies of New England to be mindful of "the need the Government has for tar, masts, deals, etc.," and to consider "how they may remove all possible obstructions to the importation of the same from the plantations."[20]

The Royal Navy actively began to order masts from New England to ensure a constant supply. Though they were more expensive than those from the Baltic, they were more reliable. Most of the time. English agents worried about their arrival. Samuel Pepys, a Member of Parliament and an acquisitions agent for the Royal Navy, wrote in early December 1666: "There is also the very good newes come of four New-England ships come home safe to Falmouth with masts for the King; which is a blessing mighty unexpected, and without which, if for nothing else, we must have failed the next year. But God be praised for thus much good fortune."[21]

The Dutch continued to stem the tide of trees from the Baltics. On Christmas Eve that same December, Pepys wrote in his diary. "No news yet of Gottenburgh fleet; which makes us have some fear, it being of mighty concernment to have our supply of masts safe."[22]

With a growing economy, the people of New England needed some sort of currency to trade. England was loath to ship gold and silver across the sea, and as the business world of the colonies became more sophisticated some homegrown form of cash became necessary. Paying for a doctor's visit with a few pine boards or a chicken very quickly became anachronistic. In 1652, the authorities of Massachusetts Bay commissioned two men to set up a mint in Boston to quite literally make money.

All the old silver colonists could find—vases, sword hilts, old buckles, broken forks, cups—was brought to the mint and melted down with some South American silver bullion collected from the Spanish by English privateers. Out of this loot, John Hull and Robert Sanderson began to turn out shillings, sixpence, and threepence. (The shillings contained about 75 percent of the silver of their English equivalents and were roughly the size of today's half dollar.) Hull was directed by the Massachusetts General Court to create a coin with an inscription around the rim and a tree on one side and the date on the other. Hull liked the idea: "What better thing," he wrote, "than a tree to portray the wealth of our country?"[23]

For every twenty "pine tree" shillings he turned out, Hull was reportedly paid one. After years of minting thousands, he was a rich man. When his daughter Hannah wed Samuel Sewell, Hull dressed in a waistcoat with silver shillings for buttons. The mint master gave his new son a dowry of silver shillings—measured on a giant scale against Hannah. So the legend goes.

Colonists who pocketed a few shillings in 1670 would find that, no matter the year they were minted, they always bore the same date on the edge above the pine. Many believe the currency was not changed for clever political reasons. In 1649, Charles I was beheaded (an event some in the colonies celebrated; if there was no king, the colonies couldn't be in violation of crown dictates for turning out their own currency).

After Charles II assumed the throne, the English ordered Massachusetts's moneymaker to stop manufacturing the evergreen shillings, declaring "coyning" a "royal prerogative." Boston's rebels ignored it and kept turning out coyns for more than fifteen years.

The patience of the crown grew thin. The Bostonians thumbed their noses at Charles II at every turn. In 1661, the Puritans of the city published their Massachusetts Declaration of Rights as a reaction to the Navigation Acts. In the document they pledged allegiance to England's monarch, but they also maintained that the Massachusetts patent was "the first and main foundation" of governance in the colony.[24]

Upon hearing of the impudence of the residents of his colony across the sea, King Charles' anger only grew. He was fed up with the blatant disregard of the Navigation Acts; he was irate that the Puritans refused to allow the Church of England into Boston; he was bothered that Massachusetts bought the land of the Province of Maine from the Gorges heirs, expanding the colony's influence—and obtaining access to the pines there. And he disliked the way the colonists fought wars with the French and Indians without consulting him first, as if they were a sovereign army. They were even minting their own currency, like a sovereign land.

His loyal deputy Edward Randolph crossed the Atlantic multiple times between his arrival in 1678 and 1684 to report on these and innumerable other violations of English law he witnessed in New England. Randolph urged the king to revoke the charter of Massachusetts. Charles II liked the idea. All these grievances served to give him the excuse he needed to pursue his real agenda—he wanted more control, and more centralized control, over the ragtag band of colonies that occupied the northeast of North America. He already had a name for the new entity he envisioned—the Dominion of New England.

In 1680 he began the process by "royalizing" New Hampshire, and sent Edward Randolph permanently to the colonies as Commissioner of the Customs and Surveyor of Pines and Timbers in Maine and New Hampshire. In 1684, the king granted his pet Randolph his wish, annulling the charter of the Massachusetts Bay colony, to the outrage of Elisha Cooke Sr., the Mathers, countless Puritans, and many businessmen. By 1686, he had abolished all of the various charters that governed Rhode Island, New Hampshire, New York, and Connecticut, and he had set up the Dominion of New England and assumed royal control over the entire region, stretching from Delaware Bay in the south to Penobscot Bay in the north. Edward Randolph hand-selected men to serve as president and councilmen for Massachusetts, Maine, and New Plymouth; the king sent him help in the form of Sir Edmund Andros to act as governor.

Andros was about as well liked as the customs agent and surveyor of the pines. He'd most recently helped to put down the Monmouth Rebellion back in England, serving as an officer. The new governor was of the opinion that the colonists left behind their rights as Englishmen when they moved to America. He levied harsh taxes, placed shackles on the press, and abolished the Massachusetts legislature—laws were instead made by the "Governor and the Council."

The Council of New England had been formed in 1685 to serve as a local legislature—Randolph and several other English authorities were made members. Many of the leading figures in the city were asked to join—most refused. These included several timber titans of New Hampshire, who were irate that the woodlands in which they worked were granted to Robert Mason by royal charter. They continued to cut them anyway—and they continued to ship masts to trading partners with addresses outside of Great Britain.

The New Hampshire loggers and Boston burghers fought constantly with Andros. John Andrew Doyle, an English historian, wrote of the governor and his methods: "All those devices of tyranny which England had resisted, even where they were rare and the exception, were now adopted as part of the regular machinery of government."[25] To make sure that the colonists played along nicely, the crown sent two companies of redcoats to Boston to be garrisoned.

The move only increased the anti-crown sentiment. Bostonians were livid, and considered the move a gross overreach of power.

Thus came the mob.

Edward Randolph and Edmund Andros spent ten months languishing in the dark confines of the Boston Gaol, and the hated Dominion of New England died while they were inside. In prison, Randolph heard news that the French and Indians had moved on Maine. When the British officials were captured the previous April, their men, stationed at frontier outposts in Wells, Kennebunk, Saco, Casco Bay, and along the Kennebec, all withdrew, leaving a big English vacuum in Maine. The French and their native allies were only too happy to move into it, sacking homes in York and running off colonists the length of the coast. This, of course, prevented access to the pines.

Randolph wrote to London about the event, dismayed that they were now cut off from the very trees that brought them there in the first place. "The fisheries and lumber (our principal commodities) are quite destroyed, besides the loss of fruitful country; all the masts for the Royal Navy are in the hands of the French and Indians."

Edward Randolph and Governor Andros stewed in lockup. There was nothing they could do to affect things. The colonists eventually were persuaded to free the captive British officials on orders of King William III, who assumed the throne when James II was deposed. Several prominent Boston men—who had been behind this minor coup, this mini revolution—were selected to represent Massachusetts in England and make the case for a new charter.

Edward Randolph fled back to England. But it wasn't long before he returned to North America, this time with an even loftier title—Surveyor General for all of North America. He spent years traveling up and down the East Coast and to the Bahamas, enforcing trade laws and winning new enemies all the while. He sailed for England again, and worked in the British Parliament to fight against new charters in the colonies.

Massachusetts won its new royal charter in 1691 to replace the one that the crown felt was too in favor of Puritans and rebels like Elisha Cooke Sr. Buried within the new document was some interesting language, which demonstrated just how important the pines of New England had become to the English: ". . . for better providing and furnishing of Masts for our Royal Navy wee do hereby reserve to us . . . ALL trees of the diameter of 24 inches and upward at 12 inches from the ground, growing upon any soils or tracts of land within our said Province or Territory not heretofore granted to any private person. We . . . forbid all persons whatsoever from felling, cutting or destroying any such trees without the royal license from us."

All pines over two feet in diameter—the prime trees in the forest—now belonged to the king.

CHAPTER FIVE

The Case of Cooke

It is to him we may look as the man who was responsible for
keeping alive the spark of revolt, who fanned the flame,
*   adding*
more fuel from day to day, creating a movement which spread
*   beyond*
the bounds of the Massachusetts Bay, engulfing the united
populace of the Atlantic seaboard in an organized, fervent
fight for the control of their own destinies.
                    —LEE EDWARD PYNE ON ELISHA COOKE JR.

IN EARLY 1718, PROMINENT BOSTON LAWYER, LEGISLATOR, AND judge Elisha Cooke was readying himself for the court case to end all court cases. It was one of those landmark, history-on-a-precipice legal battles—if the Boston legislator won, it would mean the revolution had come early to northern New England.

Elisha Cooke grew up hearing about the abuses of the English king at the kitchen table. His father, Elisha Cooke Sr., was the Speaker of the House of Massachusetts—and a notorious anti-crown activist, rallying the people of Boston and the government of Massachusetts in protest of many of the king's policies. Cooke Sr. had been part of the band of rebels who brought down the hated Dominion of New England, and defended the Massa-chusetts Charter in 1689.

Cooke Sr., a physician by trade and legislator by calling, felt strongly about the Charter of Massachusetts and the rights it granted the Commonwealth's citizens, and he made his voice heard whenever he felt any one of those rights was trod upon by the overstepping English monarch. The new charter may not have been perfect, and included much language they didn't like, but at least they were Massachusetts again and not part of some made-up royal hodgepodge. Cooke, and many others, consid-ered self-governance, to the degree that it was allowed, one of the greatest aspects of a charter. Under the direct control of the Dominion, there was none.

Cooke Sr. rose to power when Randolph and Andros were arrested, serving on the rebel council after the toppling of the Dominion, and was occasionally referred to as the "Oliver Crom-well of New England." After the crown officials were arrested, Eli-sha Cooke Sr. was among the delegation that traveled to England to represent the colonies.[1] None of this made him a popular figure among the king's men. But he didn't like them much, either.

His son, Elisha Jr., went to Harvard, just as he did, graduat-ing in 1697. The younger Cooke followed a similar career path, as well, studying medicine and becoming a physician after leav-ing school, but soon began to prefer a career in politics, striding right into governance in Boston and rising up the ranks. He quickly completed his education in law, taking a job in 1702 as Clerk of the Superior Court of Boston. (Cooke would hold the office until 1718, when his famous mouth got him in trouble with Governor Shute.)

Cooke worked with Samuel Adams, Sr., father of the Sam Adams who would become an internationally known figure during the Revolutionary War, in the "popular party" of Boston, which resisted crown encroachment in the colonies. They may as well have named the party after Cooke, because he was immensely popular around the city and in the House of Representatives. So great was the favor with which Cooke was seen by his colleagues that Governor Shute felt he had to abolish the whole legislative body because its members sided with Cooke against him. According to one historian, Elisha Cooke Jr. "contributed more than anyone else to public life in Boston."[2]

Elisha Cooke Jr. was also one of the wealthiest men in the city, with a net worth valued at more than £63,000, a spectacular sum equivalent to more than $10 million these days. He made a healthy chunk of that money among the white pines of the Province of Maine. Cooke was a heavy investor in sawmills and timber. He didn't spend a lot of time north of the Piscataqua River, however; he was an inveterate Bostonian, owner of the Goat Tavern on King Street, where he spent a lot of time drinking and scheming—but his presence was hugely felt in the woods. And he had no use for the law that gave the king rights to any trees over twenty-four inches. While he had commercial reasons to dislike the law, he genuinely considered it an affront to the rights of colonists, another instance of a faraway king trampling over his subjects.

The institution of the White Pine Act in 1711 doubled down on the language in the new Charter of Massachusetts, passed twenty years earlier. Called "An Act for the Preservation of White and other Pine trees growing in Her Majesty's Colonies . . . for the masting of Her Majesty's Navy," the new law extended the prohibitions of the Massachusetts charter to the woods of Maine, New Hampshire, and all the way down to New Jersey. The first of the so-called White Pine Acts of Parliament, it was proposed by the embittered Surveyor of the King's Woods John Bridger, and reserved for the queen's use "any White or other sort of Pine-Tree fit for Masts, not being the Property of any private Person, such Tree being of the Growth of Twenty four Inches Diameter and upwards at Twelve Inches from the Earth."[3]

The act only affected trees on lands that weren't private, but the notion of private land was a convoluted one in the English colonies of North America. Ownership of acreage was a tricky conceit because all settlements were essentially based in the feudal tradition dating back to William the Conqueror in 1066. The king granted the charters to the land—his land—on the basis that the settlers would be his vassals and would work the land in the best interest of the crown. If they didn't, by rights the king could reclaim his land. Many of the roots of the revolution could be traced back to this idea.

Deeds had been drawn up and parcels sold by New Englanders ever since they arrived, but, because surveying was primitive and records were poorly kept, property bounds were murky business. The fact that the finest pines were on lands outside bounded towns only compounded the confusion.

The White Pine Act outraged woodcutters, and especially Elisha Cooke, who offered his services as an attorney to anyone brought to trial for violating it. In 1718, he began his biggest case. The case was one of the first major steps toward independence made by the colonists, and it was all about the trees. If Cooke won, the crown would be cut off from its supply of masts from northern New England.

The facts of the case were these: The surveyor General had seized a pile of pine logs larger than twenty-four inches in diameter during a raid in the Maine woods outside of Kittery and was following the usual protocol—he was going to sell them and keep the monies for the crown. Cooke asked that the Massachusetts General Court revoke the action in the name of the province, stating that the king had no rights to the land in Maine, as it was a private property that had been purchased from Massachusetts in 1677 by the heirs of Sir Ferdinando Gorges, who held the original grant. This made the surveyor general, in essence, a trespasser. It was a bold move, and a clever interpretation of the law. And it had basis in fact.

In August 1622, a couple years after the Plymouth colony really began to take shape, King James I had granted rights to the territory to the north, known as the Province of Maine, to his loyal subjects Sir Ferdinando Gorges and John Mason. Typical of the time, the grant was rather vague, giving title to land never before surveyed, a wilderness unknown by the grantor and at least one of the grantees, with bounds as hard and fast as pencil marks on a map. The land was described as being between the Merrimac and the Kennebec rivers, the ocean, and "the river of Canada."[4]

Elisha Cooke knew the region better than both Gorges and Mason and he knew the intricacies of the law, as well. While serving as a justice of the Suffolk County Court, Cooke used his seat on the bench to undermine the admiralty courts, accusing it of "unjustly and extorsively" levying fees,[5] and he understood very well why the English wanted the trees.

During King William's War, yet another conflict with the French and their Indian allies, the French had begun preying again on English commercial ships in European waters, making Baltic masts less predictable and much more expensive, just as they had been during the Dutch Wars. In 1694, the English government asked for some samples from the colonies, and the colonists, eager to find more outlets for their timber, packaged up a shipment and sent it across the Atlantic.

Inspectors from the Royal Navy were not impressed, calling the masts "of so infirm a nature as not to be fit for use in His Majesty's ships," and they basically turned their attention back toward Riga. But the French privateers forced their hand. Stores of masts were getting low, and the British government decided to do a little research on its own. Maybe the masts sent over were damaged in the shipping? Or perhaps they didn't represent the quality on hand in the woods of New England? The Royal Navy would send their own men across the sea and into the forests.

The Privy Council, a body of advisers to the king, selected four agents to evaluate the woodlands of the colonies, primarily Maine, Massachusetts, and New Hampshire. They were given their brief: "Whereas it would be great advantage to this kingdom if its navies could be supplied from His Majesties Plantations and Colonies in America with such commodities as are imported from the East country and other foreign ports, you are in the first place to understand that your voyage to New England is for the introduction of a trade with that country for what naval materials it can produce, qualified for His Majesties Service."

And off they went.

When they arrived in Boston the four men found that the governor of New York, Massachusetts, and New Hampshire, the Irishman Richard Coote, Earl of Bellomont, wanted to be part of the club. He essentially attached himself to them, aiding them in their mission. There was a great irony to Bellomont's desire to participate—he had very recently gone to battle with the Naval Board, challenging the twenty-four-inch policy and England's right to claim the timbers he wanted to use on his estate. And now he wanted to be making and enforcing similar policy. He very much believed that the vast forestlands of his new bailiwick could supply England with all the masts and pitch it needed.[6]

The quartet—and the eager Lord Bellomont—convinced the Royal Navy that the colonies not only had pines fit for masting but plenty of them. They also discovered many violations of the twenty-four-inch rule. Edward Randolph's successor as Surveyor of Pines and Timber in Maine and New Hampshire, Jahleel Brenton, was more concerned about his duties as a customs agent than he was in the goings-on in the remote woodlands and had spent little time on enforcement. The result was that the sawmills of New England were thick with trees bearing the king's broad arrow, three hatchet marks indicating that a tree had been selected for the Royal Navy. And not only that, Boston was still sending ship after ship filled with masts to England's rivals Spain and Portugal.

The lumbermen of New Hampshire were among the worst violators—and the most difficult to corral. The woods of the White Mountains were worlds away from the streets of Boston—

and even the port of Portsmouth—and the men who worked there had little patience for the king and his little hatchet marks.

The land of New Hampshire was owned by Randolph's brother-in-law, Robert Mason, who came to the region in 1680 to look over his fiefdom. He didn't last long. The treecutters working on his land were none too keen to see him, and he was harassed and intimidated and basically run out of town, boarding a ship for London soon after he'd arrived in North America. He wanted no part of New Hampshire and was ready to sell his holdings to the first buyer.

That was Edward Cranfield, who was appointed royal governor of New Hampshire in 1682. He was as popular as Mason and Randolph and Andros before him. He fingered businessmen who chose to ignore the Navigation Acts, many of whom were Boston Puritans who had no use for Anglicans.

Cranfield incensed these men even further by trying to make the Church of England the official religion of New Hampshire. He levied taxes on vessels coming in to the Piscataqua and also on the general public, and he did so unilaterally, without the support of the assembly. In other words, without representation. He lasted three years before pressure from colonists drove him all the way to the West Indies. Toward the end of his tenure he wrote the Lords of Trade and Plantations: "I am obliged to make use of my license to go to Barbados or Jamaica, being much indisposed here."

After Randolph and Cranfield came John Bridger. By the turn of the eighteenth century the woods, as people like Randolph pointed out, were getting out of hand in the eyes of the British. Violations of the twenty-four-inch law were rampant—one 1700 survey turned up over fifteen thousand instances. Bridger was announced as surveyor general in 1705, and he was amazed at the number of transgressions he found cruising the forests of New England. He complained to his supervisor that his salary barely covered the expenses required to do his duties, because of the size of the region and the fact that he needed an armed guard to accompany him.

"The Woods are large," he wrote, "and of great extent." The people within were either savages or cutting illegally, and no one was ever punished, "for all the People here are Equally Guilty." Bridger all but begged for help, for able deputies to assist him. "I want to Catch them or at least to Watch them; here everyone's hand is against anything belonging to her Majestie or her Intrest."[7]

Bridger was an activist at the job, and he eventually got his help, sending out men to mark timber and seize oversize trees. When sawyers were caught with illegal timber he saw to it they were summarily prosecuted.

This, of course, ran Bridger afoul of Elisha Cooke.

The popular Boston legislator didn't like the new surveyor general, the feeling was mutual, and they did whatever they could to make life difficult for each other. Two men testified that Cooke was shooting his mouth off at a get together at Captain Archibald Macphreadis's house in Portsmouth. Samuel Plaisted told crown officials that Cooke, perhaps with a few cups of ale in him, as he was wont, said that the "neither the King nor [Surveyor General] Mr. Bridger his office have anything to do in the County of Yorke formerly the Province of Maine." Cooke called Plaisted "a Blockhead"[8] if he carried out the mast-inspecting duties he was deputized to do.

Macphreadis corroborated Plaistead's story. He said Cooke told him that he was going to Maine to "let Inhabitants know that they may goe on with their Logging." Ever the lawyer, Cooke told the lumbermen he knew of "no Power that Mr. Bridger has in that Province to hinder any person to cut Loggs where they please," and that if any crown official came after them, Cooke would "bare them harmless."[9]

The people were listening. Timber cutters took comfort from Cooke's promise and continued felling as they saw fit. Surveyor General Bridger was dismayed. He heard from one of his spies, who told him under "Promise of Reward in money," that there were many men felling pines with unanimity in Maine. They were dropping "a great number of Mast Trees in his Majesty's woods," and sawing them into planks, joists, and boards. These scoundrels, he said, were multiplying in the woodlands of the province, "building Saw Mills on every River and Brook almost which will soon destroy those Fine Trees."[10] The woods were "now threatened on every Side, as well as the Officer." Bridger felt he had to tread lightly. The new settlers were proving difficult to deal with, "perswaded that his Majesty has no right to the Woods in this countrey by Elisha Cook."[11]

And it wasn't just the brave tree cutters up north who were swayed by Cooke's rhetorical powers. He had a lot of friends in the House of Representatives in Massachusetts, and the issue of the king's pines was always a hot one: "for upon no other subject than the timber was the House more sensitive,"[12] wrote one observer. Governor Shute whined to the Board of Trade that the "main drift of the House" was to convince the people that the crown had no right to their woods."[13]

Bridger confronted one of Cooke's congressional allies in 1718, handing him a pair of acts of Parliament passed "for the Preservation of His Majesties Woods here in N. America." And the surveyor general was put right in his place. The councilor answered "very smartly" that acts of Parliament "were of No force with them they had a Charter."[14]

Bridger wrote later that he feared Cooke—whom he referred to as "ill-minded," "vile," "disloyal," and "malicious"—was winning over many in the colony. "The majority" of Representatives, he wrote, "are for him and his Rebellious Assertions, saying that they bought the Province of Main for £1250."[15] In other words, the woods of Maine were private property and no place for the crown.

The surveyor general found that many magistrates at the local level saw things the way Cooke saw things. Many of the mill owners of New Hampshire had a great deal of political clout and were able to lean on judges and control the outcomes of trials. In 1731, they even had the courts moved from Portsmouth to their own jurisdictions—Exeter, Hampton, and Dover.[16] The Board of Trade noticed, of course, writing at one point that it would be "very difficult if not impracticable to find a Jury who would give an impartial verdict," because those towns were the "Chief Seats of the Loggers or Woodcutters," who gave "great Encouragement to the Destruction of Your Majesty's Woods."

Bridger was often overruled and occasionally had to bear a tongue lashing for overstepping his bounds. His letters back to England and to the admiralty courts continued to be filled with pleas for support.

It was in this context that Cooke made his case. He tied up the courts for years, much to the consternation of his enemies, but the English had the final word. The crown's barristers argued that, yes, the charter for Maine was lawfully passed down to the heirs of Sir Ferdinando Gorges. But no sale of any kind in England—and the colonies were subject to English law—could "take away the King's prerogative."[17] Council for the king also emphasized to the crown how important it was for the Royal Navy to have access to the pineries of Maine.

"But Indeed I should not have made Use of any Argument of this Nature did I not think the Maintaining the Royall prerogative in Relation to the Navall Stores in America of the Utmost Consequence to the Kingdome,"[18] wrote Richard West to the Lord Commissioners of Trade and Plantations.

Cooke wasn't one to give up, and he simply came at the problem from a different direction. In 1721, backed by the Massachusetts General Court, he argued that the crown claimed rights to timber fit for masts but not to pine logs cut to twenty-foot lengths. Those, of course, should belong to the province. It was common practice in the woods of Maine and New Hampshire and Massachusetts to fell large trees—which would have been mast material—and quickly saw them into sections, rendering them no longer suitable for the Royal Navy. This tack didn't work either, but the crown grew weary of constant legal battles. They had many difficulties getting convictions—magistrates were often sympathetic to timber cutters, private property was difficult to define, witnesses might go into hiding or sit mum on the stand—and decided to simply rewrite the law.

The English had another problem. While all this was going on, Cooke was quietly at work on another method of trying the crown's patience—he was buying up land. The queen refused to relinquish rights to Maine and its trees, so Cooke figured he'd test the "private" clause of the White Pine Act from a more personal level. He acquired two grants near Pemaquid, encompassing thousands of acres. Cooke very cleverly bought acreage with the best timberlands far outside the bounds of towns. Several other Boston-based nabobs—a group of affluent land speculators that would become known as the Great Proprietors—saw what he was doing and did the same. Soon, there was a flurry of activity in the pine woods along the coast, and everyone was interested in old and lost grants, buying their own little kingdoms. They made deals with natives, set up purchases from the province, and elbowed out other investors.

The crown knew it had to do something, before all those trees were removed from its jurisdiction. If these men bought the rights to the land, they held the rights to the pines as private property. At the very least, Cooke could give them new headaches in the courts.

The Board of Trade passed a new law.

In 1722, the Naval Stores Act brought new language to the crown's fight to keep the pines. The new law repealed the White Pine Act and replaced it with one that required permission to cut "any white pine trees, not growing within any township."

Confident in Cooke, the locals continued to hew away. They also most certainly took comfort in the fact that in 1718, the year of the popular legislator's case, Surveyor General John Bridger was removed from his post. So dismayed was Bridger that he volunteered to guard the king's pine for two more years for free. "'Tis very hard," he complained to his superiors, "to serve the King all my life and at last to want bread and do the Duty." According to Bridger, lumbermen dropped more than 120 trees without a license on behalf of naval commissioner John Taylor in the year after he left his job. The navy had requested a ship's worth of masts and Taylor's men felled enough to fill six, taking advantage of the lack of oversight. "It was easier for one man to preserve the woods five years ago," Bridger wrote "than it would be for five men now."[19]

Lumbermen were felling trees with fury all along the coast of Maine, too. "To the eastward at York, Wells, Keinbank, Saco, Scarborough, Cascobay, Keinbeck, and Pemquid they cut and saw at pleasure and send them where they please," wrote a loyalist in Portsmouth in 1747.

That would have pleased Elisha Cooke Jr.—if he had been around to see it. But the stress of the job simply got to him. The constant battles he fought on behalf of the people of Massachusetts began to take their toll on the savvy legislator, and he died in 1737 at the young age of fifty-nine. His passing was marked by the entire city. The guns were fired from the battery on Long Wharf and the vessels in the harbor lowered their flags to half-staff in memorial.[20]

CHAPTER SIX

The Mast Trade

*The Act for prohibiting the cutting of white Pines, invented
on Pretence of preserving them for the Use of the Navy, has
proved the Destruction of many noble Trees fit for Masts.*
                          —BENJAMIN FRANKLIN, 1770[1]

WHEN THOMAS WESTBROOK MOVED HIS BUSINESS FROM
Portsmouth, New Hampshire, to Falmouth, Province of Maine,
in 1727, his first action was to build a fort. The small community
on Casco Bay was a wild outpost on the frontier of civilization
with danger in the trees, and few people knew this better than
the fifty-two-year-old New Hampshire native. Like so many
other early colonists, Westbrook had plied many trades by the
time he settled on the Stroudwater River in what is today Portland, Maine. The son of a Portsmouth farmer, he'd run a tavern,
worked in public government, and been a ranger during Queen
Anne's War (the second of the series of conflicts known as the
French and Indian Wars in the British colonies in North America), sent on scouting missions into enemy territory. His service
in the militia had led him to be commissioned first a captain and
later a colonel and placed in charge of "the East," those dark and
menacing woods to the north of Boston that were filled with
native braves and French war bands.

Five years before relocating to Maine, Westbrook had distinguished himself in the fight against the French and their Indian allies by leading a winter raid against the Abenaki at Norridgewock. The English suspected Father Sebastian Rale, a Jesuit priest, of very un-Christian behavior—instigating the native attacks that had been happening at settlements along the coast, where the burning of homes and the kidnapping of those colonists brave—or foolish—enough to live on the very northern edge of English territory were everyday occurrences.

The colonel was charged with bringing Rale to justice, and he and three hundred soldiers marched to the native stronghold, ninety miles north of Falmouth, on snowshoes, carrying all of their supplies on their backs, and surrounded the Abenaki encampment while most of the Indians were away hunting. The priest had taken to the woods and was in hiding when he heard of the English advance, and the colonel and his men ransacked his cabin, making off with the Jesuit's strongbox. Inside were papers that proved just what those in Boston had suspected—Rale was the one planning and coordinating the campaign of terror on the English. (A few years later, the priest was executed along with dozens of natives, including women and children, in yet another colonial raid on Norridgewock, and his scalp was reportedly paraded through the streets of Boston.)

All this was surely in the back of Westbrook's mind when it came time to move his base of operations from Portsmouth to Falmouth, and he made sure to build a defensible position. The colonel had been appointed a royal mast agent, the middleman between the lumbermen who worked the forest and Her Majesty's Royal Navy. This was a station of great importance and stature—just as much, perhaps, as being in charge of the Maine militia. One of the reasons the English were working so hard to claim these woods and waters was because they were filled with easily accessible white pines. The tall conifers grew all along riverbanks—and far inland, deep into native territory—and the

Royal Navy wanted them badly—by the early eighteenth century the English had decided it was an issue of national security to secure the bounty of the New England forest.

Colonel Thomas Westbrook's migration eastward was symbolic of a shift in the industry. Portsmouth had been the busiest and most important port for the lucrative mast trade in the colonies, with a steady stream of white pine spars flushing down the wide Piscataqua River. Once the pines near Portsmouth had been felled, cutters moved up the streams and rivers that fed the mighty waterway, and soon the forests were thin on the Cocheco, Bellamy, Oyster, Lamprey, and Salmon Falls, too. The navy's contractors found themselves traveling farther and farther afield to find groves of pines, and the Falmouth area was seen as an ideal alternative. Many rivers sluiced their way to the deepwater port at Casco Bay, perfect for carrying masts. And the surrounding woodlands were full of tall, stately *Pinus strobus*.

The *New England Weekly Journal* heralded the change in the pine trade in 1727: "We have an account that the mast business, which has for some time been so much benefit of the neighbor province of New Hampshire, is removed further eastward, where it has been carried on the last winter with such success as could hardly have been expected."

A year later, Ralph Gulston, the Royal Navy's biggest mast contractor in Maine, said basically the same thing. He fervently recommended an official fort be built on Casco Bay, because "the great waste" of "white Pine Trees, in the Province of Newhampshire in New England (from whence the Royal Navy was formerly Supplyed with Masts) I found it impracticable now to get them there."[2]

Colonel Westbrook was all too happy to oblige. He was right in the thick of things, with pitch all over his hands. He'd been working in the mast trade in Portsmouth since as early as 1721, using some of his wealth to invest in the Muscongus (Waldo) Patent, which covered a vast territory between the Muscongus and Penobscot rivers. (The broad, beautiful Penobscot was often considered the de facto boundary between the English holdings to the west and south and the French territory to the north and east.) Before moving, he'd set up a lumber camp a few miles from Stroudwater on the Fore River and began dropping trees.

In 1727, he became one of a relative few permanent "citizens" of Falmouth, shortly after receiving his appointment as a royal mast agent, and he chose a quiet, sixty-nine-acre lot on a hill where the Stroudwater River flows into the Fore as the site of his home, Harrow House. Then he built a fifteen-foot-high stockade and a garrison and trained gun emplacements on the river. The location was ideal for collecting masts in the protected Fore River before moving them down the wide saltwater way to the docks at Falmouth, and it had the hydraulics for sawmills, which could extract sellable boards and beams from waste pine. This lumber could in turn be used for building homes right on the neck at Falmouth, which, thanks to the mast trade and the quieting of Indian raids, was beginning to grow.

Falmouth was, in fact, sprouting like a new sapling. The mast trade was prosperous and lucrative, as the residents of New Hampshire had discovered. The industry was the largest money-maker for the northern colonies, eclipsing even fishing, and it had an imprimatur that was unmatched—by this time, the English knew that their navy was the key to becoming the superpower they wanted to be and that they could no longer rely solely on their European sources of naval stores. Thanks to this, the mast trade was backed by law, unlike most other industries, which gave it the potential to be extraordinarily profitable. And the colonists were all too happy to supply masts to Portugal, Spain, Holland, and even the French on occasion.

Thomas Westbrook had seen the potential of the industry early. In 1721 he traveled to Boston to throw in his lot—in the form of about £300—with the Lincolnshire Proprietors, a group of investors who held the Muscongus Patent, thirty-six square miles of woodlands between the Muscongus and Penobscot rivers. The "thirty associates" represented something of a who's who of Boston at the time, including future governor Thomas Hutchinson, Adam Winthrop, a military captain and scion of the influential Winthrop family, and future mast agent John Wentworth. They were among those spurred to buy land in Maine by Elisha Cooke and his battle with the Brits. One of the first decisions was to elect Westbrook a captain, and to build a fort at what is now Thomaston,[3] where George Weymouth had gone ashore the century before.

All of these Boston merchants were certainly on to something. The soil of the Province of Maine was ideal for nurturing seedlings, and *Pinus strobus* proliferated. (Even today, driving north on the Interstate from New Hampshire to Maine, the change in the character of the woodlands becomes stark.)

There was just the small matter of finding the right trees in this fastness—only one in ten thousand would do. Masts for His Majesty's Navy had to come from the finest pines in the forest— this meant extraordinarily tall, straight as a line level, and free of decay. Mast agents—or more likely their hired woods cruisers— would spend days and weeks exploring, climbing tall trees to look out over the forest canopy for likely specimens. When they found one that had potential, they would bat the base with an ax handle to see if the interior was weak with rot. If the tree was solid, the blow made a heavy, fat, thud; if its core were starting to decay it would often sound hollow or reverberant. Once a quantity of worthy boles had been selected, usually found in isolated stands, woodsmen would, as they put it, go a'masting.

Extricating something 110 feet tall, 3 feet wide, and weighing 18 tons, surrounded by tall, intractable obstructions, was a chore—the most precarious of games of pickup sticks—and the trees had to arrive at the mast yard undamaged. Many a fine trunk was destroyed in the process of felling—cracking on hidden rocks, snapping on other trees—and bringing them down had to be done very, very carefully. By hand. Axes were the weapon of choice, saws came into use later, at the yard, and the trees had to hit the ground just so.

In the best-case scenario, the mast agent found a perfect pine on a riverbank so that it could be simply felled into the water and floated to big mast pools for collection. But most of the time, the mast pines were singled out in some grove deep in the woodlands, surrounded by other tall trees. The neighboring trees were dropped first and either stacked in a bed to cushion the fall of the king's trunk or removed to allow the pine to crash onto a thick mattress of snow. The ground underneath any snow cover had to be checked for submerged boulders, tall stumps, or anything else that could damage the mast. Often huge piles of snow or leaves would be moved to pad the ground and soften the blow. The stump left behind after the tree was felled would be as wide as a dining room table.

Once prostrate, the tree was limbed and readied for removal. Often, new "mast roads" would have to be cut, wide swaths of cleared forest that allowed for huge turning radiuses. (These thoroughfares would encourage later settlement, and many became central arteries for their communities—from North Carolina to Maine there are hundreds of towns and cities with streets named Mast Road. Some New England towns still have triangular town squares, set up to allow for the wide sweep of masts.) Swampers would mow a broad path through the woods, cutting tangly underbrush, dragging out rocks, filling in holes, and creating a corridor that teamsters could work. Beasts of burden, sometimes horses, usually oxen, were then hooked to the long bole along with wheels as tall as eighteen feet called galamanders. Then they began balking.

A prominent resident of Boston marveled at the extrication of a relatively slender king's pine on the Salmon Falls River in New Hampshire, writing: "rode into a swamp to see a mast drawn of about 26 inches or 28; about two and thirty oxen before, and about four yoke by the side of the mast between the fore and hinder wheels. 'Twas a notable sight."[4]

Larger spars would require bigger teams of oxen, sometimes close to a hundred animals. In the winter, teamsters would pull masts on sledges, "twitching" them out of the woods. It was heavy, dangerous work. Masts could weigh in excess of thirty-five thousand pounds, and, being round, there was always the danger of them rolling. Hills, vales, boulders, brooks, other trees—the sundry obstacles of the woods—only heightened the risk. Even with teamsters at the front and back and ropes and slub lines on the sides, hazards were ever present.

Depending upon where they were felled, masts were yarded to huge piles beside rivers to be pushed in when the ice went out. In the spring, they were driven downstream to mast pools on the coast. When the pines reached their saltwater destination, they were inspected for flaws by yard bosses. Those that didn't make the cut—the Royal Navy didn't accept anything less than perfect—ended their days as boards and lumber. Selected trees were moved to a "mast house," where mastwrights went to work, transforming trunks into masts, using axes and adzes and draw shaves. These craftsmen removed remaining limbs and bark, made the pole smooth, and gave it the sixteen sides the Royal Navy specified.

As loads of expertly sculpted masts became ready they were moved to the shore, where they were loaded onto "mast ships," which had the privilege of flying the King's Jack. Huge cargo vessels—sometimes as large as a thousand tons, but typically four hundred tons—these transports had rear doors that could be opened to make a difficult process easier. Ships often took as many as fifty masts aboard, filling the hull, and it made for heavy sailing.

"Our old vessel shipped many seas," wrote one seaman in 1785, "being bound up with spars was not as lively as with another cargo."[5] Once under way, the mast ships sailed for the Royal Navy mast pools in Portsmouth, Plymouth, and Deptford, England, almost always as part of a convoy protected by British warships. Also onboard would be bags filled with correspondence for English eyes. For a time these deliveries were as regular as the mail—as one New Hampshire historian put it: "The mast fleet were the couriers of the sea, the surest and quickest means of communication between the two continents."[6]

From surveyors and timber cruisers to fellers and road crews, from teamsters to river drivers, yard bosses to shipwrights, guards and longshoremen, to the captain and crew of mast ships, the mast industry was huge, employing thousands. Not to mention the lumbermen, papermakers, furniture craftsmen, coopers, and shingle and clapboard makers in all of the various trades that benefited in a less direct way. The mast agent was at the center of this circus, orchestrating everything. He contracted crews, inspected masts, hired transport, and made arrangements with the Royal Navy.

Though controversy swirled in the woodlands, thanks to the arguments of men like Elisha Cooke, many were happy to fulfill the Royal Navy's orders—it was a very lucrative business. In 1767, an August op-ed in the New Hampshire *Gazzette* argued as much, making the case for enforcement of the broad arrow laws: "Especially when all that is required of us is to preserve such trees as nature has provided for the sole use of the Navy, and which the laws of our country enjoin upon us, for falling a sacrifice to the avaricious and unbounded desires of groveling and mean spirited men."[7]

Bringing this new industry to the wilds of Falmouth was no small thing—some historians have compared it to the oil business that would emerge in later centuries. Money had been flowing through Portsmouth like sap through a tree. A report to the English Board of the Trade showed just how valuable pine exports had become to the community on the Piscataqua. In 1718–1719, just as Colonel Thomas Westbrook was getting into the business, Portsmouth shipped 199 masts, 520 spars, and 151 bowsprits. And that's just "mastidge." They also shipped 644 pine planks and 915,331 feet of boards (pine and spruce would be most likely).

This in addition to 80,950 barrel staves, 11,000 clapboards, 55,472 feet of joists, and 5,515 feet of square timber, much of which would have been pine.[8]

This was big business. Masts were fetching top dollar—or rather, top pounds. A single thirty-six-inch mainmast sold to the Naval Board for about £130 sterling in 1720—which is more than $25,000 by today's dollars. The Royal Navy had taken 637 masts from New Hampshire alone between 1712 and 1718.[9]

Of course, most of the money made its way into the pockets of business owners, contractors, and mast agents. Power was very much top down, and the holders of Royal Navy commissions were from the highest heights of English society, men with their lips to the king's ear. Just as defense contractors are embroiled in politics today, the men at the top of the mast tree were able to consolidate their power and construct a virtual monopoly with the help of Parliament and the monarchy. At the end of the seventeenth century one man, Sir William Warren, held most of the contracts for the Royal Navy Board.[10] Warren had a large timber yard in Wapping, outside London, and thanks to his friends in high places, he processed almost all of the masts in England. When people decried this as a monopoly, Samuel Pepys, a Member of Parliament who bought masts, working closely with Warren, countered that the Naval Board was not in the business of spreading favors.[11] Later in life Warren began to share the wealth a little, involving junior partners, and at the time of his death, most of the mast contracts in New England were in the hands of William Gulston, John Henniker, and the firm of Durand and Bacon. Political wrangling, bribes, nepotism—the dark arts of high finance—all occurred as they tried to maintain control of their market share.

Underneath these men were the mast agents, who were very much at their mercy. Thus Colonel Westbrook was beholden to Samuel Waldo who was beholden to the Royal Naval Board. There were only a handful of mast agents in the colonies, and the position was freighted with power, though they were not crown officials. They were simply North America–based contractors—"licensees of licensees permitted to harvest the crown timber,"[12] as historian S.F. Manning put it—but they did carry the weight of the king behind them. According to most records, Samuel Waldo was the mast agent of Boston and Colonel Westbrook was the mast agent of Falmouth, but some historians suggest that Westbrook was something of a subcontractor to Waldo. In the woods of Maine, it didn't really matter, Westbrook was the region's most powerful figure thanks to his grip on its white pine.

Perhaps because he understood that he held a commission at the whim of another, Colonel Westbrook diversified his operations in Falmouth. He became "a large proprietor of land, built mills, employed many men and by his activity and capital, essentially promoted the prosperity of the town."[13] A large fire broke out on the coast of Maine and New Hampshire, felling a fifty-mile swath of land as effectively as any team of sawyers, before burning itself to death on Casco Bay. Many of the best trees were affected, and some mast suppliers decided to try their luck farther Down East, building new "lumbering settlements" as far as Machias. Georgetown became a center of mast production; Mount Desert Island and land along the Kennebec and Penobscot rivers, too, were tapped for their trees.[14] Even so, Westbrook's empire continued to grow, and as it did, so did Falmouth. By 1772, the community had become the colonies' largest supplier of white pine masts to the Royal Navy.

Thanks to his boss Samuel Waldo, though, Westbrook's empire would all fall apart. Like any other highly profitable business, the mast industry had a cutthroat aspect to it, and it was filled with double crossings, bribes, and other dirty dealings. History has never revealed the reason, but Westbrook and Waldo had a falling out, and in 1737 Waldo won a judgment worth more than £7,500 against Westbrook in a Boston court. The colonel protested that he had not been able to attend and defend himself.

Westbrook appealed and sued Waldo for twice that sum. The matter was tied up in courts for years.

In 1743, Waldo attacked Westbrook again, this time for the sum of £15,000, and backed by law. Like many other New Englanders to follow, the colonel was land rich and cash poor and could not pay the fee. His assets were stripped from him, and he died penniless a year later. Legend has it that Waldo wanted Westbrook's body, and that the colonel's family had to move it in the dark of night and bury it in a hidden grave to keep the unscrupulous mast agent away.

CHAPTER SEVEN

Woodcutters Revolt

The great issue began in the forests of Maine, in the contest of her Lumbermen with the King's Surveyor as to the right to cut and the property in white pine trees.
—RUFUS KING SEWALL ON THE
AMERICAN REVOLUTION[1]

ENEMIES WERE ALL AROUND HIM. COLONEL DAVID DUNBAR, the surveyor general of the king's woods in New England, saw brigands in the forests and turncoats in the highest offices in the land, and he was beginning to get scared. Where once he marched imperiously around New England, burning sawmills and evicting squatters, he was starting to feel, by the fall of 1730, that the coldness enveloping him wasn't solely due to the autumn air. He felt surrounded by people who genuinely hated him and a true menace in the air.

And he was right.

A Scots Irishman, David Dunbar had finagled his way into his job in 1728, currying favor from well-placed friends he met in England while serving in His Majesty's army. But once on the ground in New England, he saw the difficulties of enforcing the White Pine Acts, and he wrote pleading letters to his employers asking for help.

In one piece of correspondence dated October 1730, he begged of clerk Alured Popple: "Whereas under my present circumstances and difficultys, without power, mony or friends, it is imposssble for me to Strive against so much opposition & so many Enemys, & yet I will try all I can until I receive farther Orders either to be impowered or discharged."[2]

It certainly wasn't easy being a representative of King George in the northern colonies in the 1730s, especially after the Mast (or Broad Arrow) Act of 1729. That decree claimed for the crown all trees twenty-four inches in diameter at a foot off the ground, regardless of where they were located. In the earlier White Pine Acts and the Naval Stores Act, the king's woods stopped at the boundary of a private property, but now they rolled over previous deeds and purchased lands, all across New England. The only exception was acreage that changed hands before 1690, but those woods were few and far between, and private property that was "enclosed" or fenced. And everyone involved knew how practical fencing all of New England would be.

Trees claimed by the king would be marked with three strikes of the hatchet—the broad arrow—leaving behind a scar that looked like a turkey track. David Dunbar's predecessors had penetrated every forest in New England, spending days and weeks in the dark woods, looking for the finest mast trees and applying the royal mark. Surveyor General John Bridger is said to have marked six thousand trees himself. John Wentworth and John Ruggles cruised New Hampshire and Connecticut. Adolphus Benzel scouted Lake Champlain and the St. Lawrence areas, and Thomas Scammell worked the Maine coast.[3]

Some of these men found compliant citizens in the surrounding communities. Wentworth reported of his travels: "I informed the nearest & indeed all the settlers Hunters and Indians that they must be preserved for His Majesty under the severest penalty of the Law & they have all promised me to obey and notify others." Others, not so much. Thomas Scammell found rampant illegal cutting in Maine (and also claims to have seen a pine with a circumference of seventeen feet).[4] Some woodsman purposefully set Scammell on missions of folly, telling him of fictional violations and sending him in search.[5]

Scammell found many people irate about the new regulations, which were all but a declaration of war to many in New England. By the early eighteenth century, the white pine of Maine and New Hampshire was an economic powerhouse and a source of lumber for the homes going in across the region. And now a monarch three thousand miles away was claiming rights to their rightful property for his masts? Dunbar was doomed the moment he crossed the Atlantic.

Ire about the pines just added to a growing list of grievances that colonists had. The Dominion of New England had turned so many against the crown. One of Dunbar's predecessors, Lord Bellomont, who was governor of Massachusetts and New Hampshire in 1700, described the tenor of the time, explaining to his superiors back in London what it was like to meet with colonial legislators: "Three or four councilors stood up at once, and one or two asked me with some warmth what the laws of England had to do with them, and one of 'em said that they were too much cramped in their liberties already."[6]

Some other representatives of the crown were able to keep the peace—Colonel Westbrook remained a fairly popular figure in Maine, for instance. But Colonel Dunbar was in for it. Unlike the gregarious Westbrook, Dunbar was another type of character altogether. Known for his "impossibly bad temper," he was famously unfamiliar with the concept of diplomacy, preferring the blunt, straightforward approach.

Dunbar received his commission in 1728, replacing Charles Burniston, who was so scarce the locals took "no notice" of him "as if there were no such man as Surveyor General of the King's Woods," according to one of his deputies.[7] With the new law of 1729, the English government decided it was time to have a more active role on the ground, making sure that there was no illegal cutting going on. They had been apprised of the situation for decades and determined it was time to tighten the grip. Just as it had been the job of the sheriff of Nottingham to prevent hunters from taking the king's deer, it was Colonel Dunbar's task to prevent woodsmen from taking any of the king's pines.

Dunbar didn't sail for Boston immediately, however. Instead he remained in Piccadilly and sent his brother, Jeremiah, as his deputy to have a look around, instructing him to stop the cutting of a single stick of white pine. As soon as Jeremiah arrived, he realized how foolish that notion was. And, bright and capable, he also understood how difficult it would be to prevent New Englanders from harvesting whatever they wanted. He quickly saw that all the action was now taking place in Maine—and that the crown had a real problem there. A problem by the name of Elisha Cooke, who continued to be a constant irritant for colonial constables.

It also set up a grand entrance for David Dunbar, who arrived in Boston with a solution to the Maine conundrum. The Irishman told the governor of Massachusetts his plan just as soon as he disembarked in the summer of 1729, making himself enemy number one in the form of Massachusetts governor Jonathan Belcher. Belcher was incensed when Dunbar told him the vast woodlands of Maine, from the Kennebec River to the St. Croix River, a region overflowing with the most sought after of natural resources—the money-filled white pines—were no longer a part of Massachusetts. They were to become a new crown colony called Sagadahoc and annexed to Nova Scotia. Dunbar carried with him royal orders instructing him to "settle as well as to superintend and govern Sagadahoc."[8]

Using intel supplied by his brother on the ground in New England, Dunbar had hatched this land grab himself and, amazingly, was able to sell it to the crown, with the help of friends he made while serving in the English army. The legal basis he concocted was not unlike Elisha Cooke's: He claimed that the territory had been stolen from Massachusetts by the French and Indians, and that when it was retaken, it was won by the English crown, giving the king the right to do with it what he wanted. According to Dunbar and his allies, this made null and void all the previous deeds to the territory held by the Great Proprietors. He wrote to his handlers at the Imperial Board of Trade that if they recognized the claim of Massachusetts to the region, "there will be a kind of Warr 'tween these pretend proprietors and those that will go to settle upon the King's terms, for they will not quit possession."[9]

The colonel promised to settle the land himself, which pleased the crown, and to set aside three hundred thousand of the finest acres of pine as a nursery for the use of the Royal Navy. He intended to lay out cities and towns on the Sheepscot and Damariscotta rivers, and began planning the communities of Townsend, Harrington, and Walpole. None of this sat well with Governor Belcher, Elisha Cooke, or the wealthy investors who thought they held the rights to these woodlands. Belcher was absolutely irate, referring to Dunbar as "the most malicious, perfidious creature that wears human shape."

Dunbar was fully aware of the anger he caused, writing back to one of his English sponsors, the Duke of Newcastle's secretary, that he had "suffered worse treatment in New England than I had in Spain from our enemies."

Fresh off the boat, the new surveyor general was hated by the white collars. It wouldn't be long before the men who worked the forests hated him, too.

Colonel Dunbar promptly removed himself to Pemaquid, a small outpost about a third of the way up the coast of Maine, and rebuilt an old fortification there, naming it Fort Frederick. The governor of Nova Scotia sent a company of thirty soldiers to man his garrison, and Dunbar issued a proclamation to the settlements about his commission and rule. He then brought in a Nova Scotian surveyor to lay out the land, making plans for a city at Pemaquid and chopping up the countryside into two-acre lots.

And he returned to Ireland to find a crop of settlers willing to risk a new life on this rugged frontier—hardy Irishmen and women of Scottish blood, like himself, bringing back about fifty and setting them up as his tenants. Dunbar promised them title to their acreage if they built a house of at least eighteen feet and cleared their lots within three years; he also said he would help take care of them in the interim. It didn't take long for these promises to be altered and the tenants to fall out with Dunbar. They liked him about as much as the bluebloods of Boston did.

All of this, though, was secondary to Dunbar's real job as surveyor general of the king's woods. He had his hands full policing the forests and making sure settlers were complying with the Mast Act. When he wasn't building himself a fine home on the banks of the Damariscotta River, amid a grove of soaring pines, or otherwise constructing his empire, he would travel the countryside inspecting lumbering operations. He didn't have to look far. He found plenty of settlers, among them his own neighbors, with the temerity to cut the king's pines.

The area around Pemaquid was prime masting country. For almost a hundred years, woodcutters had been felling pines thereabouts, moving them down to Pemaquid for shipping. In 1684, seventeen men petitioned the governor to allow them to use the Sheepscot River as a port, instead of having to push their "sticks" so much farther downstream for pickup at Pemaquid, the area's only authorized dock station, writing, "At New Dartmouth in Ships Gutt [Sheepscot] river ar considderable inhabbitance and many more Coming and promising a Considerable trad of shiping ffor maste and Lumber."

By the time Dunbar arrived, that mast trade was well under way, and there were mills on the Sheepscot River, a pretty tidal waterway that threaded through the countryside north of Pemaquid. Many of the residents of the area, among them lumbermen, were "slow in submitting" to Dunbar's "claim and dictation," as one local historian puts it, and the colonel gave them the squeeze, threatening to evict them from their lands. "He was regardless of either ancient Grants, Deeds or actual Possessions, and resolved to bear down all opposition, and make in his own name, any conveyance by which he could make money."[10]

In September 1730, a local named Josiah Grover from New Harbor, a settlement in the Pemaquid area, wrote to the general court for help against the surveyor general and his men. He said he was returning from a fishing trip when a group of six Irishmen climbed aboard his boat "Armed with Guns and Clubbs, and in a hostile Violent Manner." The gang attempted to detain Grover "till Col. Dunbar should arrive," but the wily prisoner was able to distract his captors and make a break for it, running all the way to Boston. Other people in the area, he wrote, suffered similar treatment.[11]

Many settlers complained to Massachusetts and asked for protection from the colonel, whom they referred to as "the tyrant." The tables of the general court in Boston were said to be "crowded with petitions for Dunbar's removal."[12] None were more eager to see the surveyor general gone than Joseph Roberts, Samuel Whittemore, and Jonathan Loring, who owned and ran a lumbering operation near the Sheepscot. They claimed that Dunbar showed up with an armed guard, threatened to arrest them, forcibly evicted them from their homes and business, seized their lumber, and then torched their houses, burning them to the ground. They added their voices to the chorus of angry settlers, beseeching Massachusetts to oust Dunbar and get rid of his cooked-up colony, placing Maine back under Massachusetts's control. (Whittemore would go on to be the oldest soldier in the colonial army during the Revolution, rushing into battle at seventy-eight, sword and musket in hand.)

The outcry was heard all the way across the Atlantic, and the crown agreed to consider the case. Samuel Waldo, mast agent and one of the Great Proprietors, those investors who had put up money for acreage in Maine, the same lands Dunbar was claiming as his bailiwick, was sent to London to argue their case. The fate of Maine—and the mast trade—was in the balance. Arguments were heard on both sides, and the crown ultimately decided in August 1731 that the defeat of the French ought not to have superseded the rights of Massachusetts. Which meant Colonel David Dunbar had to go. (English officials were probably also responding to the ceiling-scraping piles of letters complaining about Dunbar.) The Colonel managed to survive in Maine for another two years before being transferred to New Hampshire.

That didn't go well, either.

When his name was put in contention for the position of lieutenant governor of the royal province of New Hampshire, the Board of Trade wrote to the Duke on his behalf: "We presume your Grace will have very few applications for that employment, which is really of little value, having no fixed salaries or any perquisites save as arise from the good will of a very poor province." And there was not much of that good will to go around. The men on the Board of Trade were keenly aware of the reputation of Dunbar at this point but they figured unpopularity went with the territory—"In New England," they wrote, "anyone who does his duty to the Crown makes enemies."[13]

Dunbar was relocated like a pedophile Catholic priest, doing the same duties just in a different place.

David Dunbar discovered plenty more enemies among the pines of New Hampshire. It wasn't long after he assumed the lieutenant governorship of the province that he found himself at the heart of another incident that precipitated the impending revolution. In addition to his new role as an assistant to the governor, he continued his work as surveyor general, and one of his proposals was to license or register sawmills so that they could be better regulated. This was wildly unpopular. Mill owners had no use for the king or his license and threated to "girdle" the trees marked by the broad arrow. Girdling entailed cutting a ring around the tree three or four inches deep to prevent sap from rising. The big pine would dry out and become too brittle for masting. But they'd be fine for boards or shingles.[14]

Tactics like this were common. The woods of New Hampshire would become famous for their "pine-tree patriots," and they became the battlefield of what would later become known as the Woodland Rebellion. Loggers generally felt that the king could take his broad arrow and shove it up his ass—rebel sentiment was rife—and for the most part they weren't worried about enforcement.

Mill owners used many crafty methods to fool surveyors. Some were simple: dump logs into the river when the crown's agents were around, or saw boards to twenty-two or twenty-three inches and dispose of the last inch. Many original houses in New Hampshire still feature beautiful wide pine boards beneath their shingles. Others were cleverer: some woodsman would mark pines they wanted with the broad arrow to frighten away rival cutters. They would dress up as natives and cut trees after dark, which led to a law forbidding anyone to cut trees wearing a disguise—under penalty of flogging.[15] They burned stands of pine, making the tall trees unsuitable for masts, and would then "salvage" the timber.

About a decade before David Dunbar arrived in New Hampshire, one of the surveyor general's deputies, Portsmouth-based Robert Armstrong, reported finding more than twenty-five thousand white pine logs in excess of the allowed twenty-four inches. He estimated that for every mast that found its way across the Atlantic, about five hundred were cut and sawn into boards and lumber by backwoods outlaws,[16] and he wrote to his supervisors that he felt in genuine danger when doing his rounds, bemoaning "the barbarous treatment officers meet with that do their duty."[17]

Surveyors general had the full weight of the crown behind them, and they had license to seize whatever they felt necessary. They collected commissions when they confiscated logs, and they had networks of informers whom they were allowed to pay with monies made from selling the taken timber. Given this sort of power, and money-making potential, bribes and extortion were sure to follow. Surveyors General Armstrong, John Bridger, and others were often accused of using gangster tactics to fill their own pockets.

And none were more hated than Colonel David Dunbar.

Just as his arrival in Massachusetts and Maine quickly went sour, he didn't take long to anger the upper echelons of New Hampshire society. For almost a decade, the official publication of the General Assembly of New Hampshire would list "not exercising his office on account of disagreement with the Governor," next to Dunbar's name. Governor Johnathan Belcher disliked Dunbar immensely, and the feeling was reciprocated. Correspondence back and forth to England is filled with each one badmouthing the other to their superiors. In one such missive, Belcher described David Dunbar as a "plague to the Governor and a deceiver of the people."[18] Belcher hated Dunbar so much that in November 1730, a Royal Order had to be issued to prevent him from taking up arms against the surveyor general. It called for a force to "restrain Governor Belcher from Military Execution against [Dunbar's] Fredericksfort."[19]

Even among his mast-agent colleagues, Dunbar was highly unpopular. The surveyor general had been warned about Samuel Waldo by his predecessor, who wrote: "It is not consistent with His Majesty's interest that mast agents and factors should erect sawmills among the pines."[20] Both Samuel Waldo and Colonel Thomas Westbrook had their own mills in the Falmouth area and made a tidy profit. Waldo and Dunbar had scrapped before. The Great Proprietors, of course, had made every effort to have Dunbar's Sagadahoc Province annulled. Dunbar referred to Waldo as "a man that has not the best character" and also as "one of Dr. Cook's Violent ones," a reference to Elisha Cooke and his crown dissenters. The pair had many dealings over the course of Dunbar's career. The surveyor general had "interrupted" a group of 120 settlers "and a minister" Waldo had sent to Maine to live and work. The surveyor general insisted the grants to the land they had were invalid—and that they had to get grants from him.

Waldo, in turn, tattled on him, signing an April 1730 petition to the Board of Trade against him.[21] Back and forth they went in a woodsy tête-à-tête.

Colonel Thomas Westbrook liked Dunbar about as much as Waldo did.

David Dunbar had had Westbrook removed from the Council at Portsmouth on the grounds that he was no longer a resident of New Hampshire, which infuriated the Maine man. Westbrook later accused Dunbar of sabotaging his efforts to fulfill a Royal Navy order. When he rebuffed an offer from Dunbar to purchase a lot of inferior masts, "a cargo of jackstaffs" as Westbrook put it, Westbrook's masting teams suddenly found they could not get their product to port, where mast ships waited at anchor for weeks. Newly cut masts were mysteriously rolled down hillsides to crack against rocks, others were sawed up into boards. Never one to shy from a confrontation, Westbrook wrote to Dunbar that he "had great reason to believe" that Dunbar had made efforts to "damnify my Interest and to intercept Mr. Ralph Gulston in his complying with his contract. What constructs can any man living make of it else; When I had so earnestly desired your particular care of ye aforesaid Timber."

The woodsmen despised Dunbar even more, and they often beat him in games of wit. When Dunbar seized a pile of twenty pine logs over the twenty-four-inch limit that were stacked outside the mill of Peter Wyre of North Yarmouth, the mill owner simply proclaimed his innocence. Despite the fact that they were on his property—Dunbar's surveyors made the point that the land wasn't even Wyre's, it was ungranted—the North Yarmouth sawyer said he had no idea how the timbers got there. They mysteriously appeared. Dunbar thought he had Wyre in a bind as tough as pine knot, and the matter went to the admiralty courts.

The judge, however, sided with Wyre. He ruled that there was no "ocular" proof that Wyre had felled the trees thus there was no way to prove he was lying and he couldn't be convicted of

the crime. Dunbar was outraged and demanded an appeal. Judge
Nathaniel Byfield granted the appeal but only on the grounds that
the surveyor general would pay treble the court costs if the appeal
proved a waste of time.

Dunbar wrote to his superiors: "I shall be a Sufferer &
Insulted if I do not Succeed."[22] He didn't succeed. Byfield again
ruled in favor of Wyre.

The judge was another old adversary of the surveyor general
and related by marriage to Governor Belcher. The judge and
Dunbar would do battle on a number of occasions, enough times
that Dunbar attempted to get him declared unfit. Dunbar argued
that this "poor superannuated Gentleman, near 80 years old, who
had already distinguished himself very Partiall to the Country . . .
ought to be removed."

Byfield, in turn, accused Dunbar of "terrorizing the people of
New England."

The enmity grew so great Dunbar even sent fraudulent court
papers to England as proof that Byfield was crooked. They arrived
too late, however. The superannuated judge passed away before
any action could be taken against him.

These kinds of actions won David Dunbar a number of death
threats. In 1734, things came to a head on two occasions. The first
was at Dover. Dunbar paid a visit to a prominent mill owner, Paul
Gerrish, and accused him of illegal cutting and then attempted
to seize pine boards as evidence. Words were exchanged, Gerrish
telling Dunbar what would happen to him if he attempted to take
the wood. Dunbar then threatened "with death" anyone who would
stand in his way. Gerrish returned the threat to Dunbar, saying he
would kill the surveyor general if he removed his property. Dunbar
decided to live another day, and the wood sat where it lay.

But the biggest event was to occur later in the year. Colonel
Dunbar heard through his various spies that a great deal of illegal
cutting was taking place in the community of Exeter, fourteen

miles south of Portsmouth near the Massachusetts border. A small village, it sat at a point where the Exeter River flowed into the tidal Squamscott and was one of the four original towns in New Hampshire. And an active band of outlaws was reportedly helping themselves to the king's woods, piling evidence of their transgressions at the Copyhold Mill. Dunbar resolved to pay these criminals a visit and surreptitiously made his way to the woodcutting operation. But when he got close, he was seen, and a litany of abuse and several gunshots were directed his way. The bullets weren't meant to harm him, only to scare him off—and they worked. The surveyor general fled, certain that illegal cutting was taking place on Exeter Stream.

When he got back to Portsmouth, Dunbar hired a crew of ten men to return to the scene. They took a boat down the Squamscott on April 23 intent on recovering the ill-gotten pine and made it to Exeter after dark, setting themselves up for the night at Gilman's Tavern on Water. The men were quite pleased with their mission—anticipating the cash they'd make upon impounding the wood—and several were enjoying Simon Gilman's ale while the others had retired for the evening.

James Pitman was in the kitchen of the tavern with his brother, Benjamin, Robert Gallaway, and Benjamin Dockum when three local men began an argument with them. The townie trio then seized Gallaway by the hair, struck him several blows, and pulled him along the floor before Pitman intervened. He screamed, "Help they will kill the man,"[23] and ran to find Colonel John Gilman, who was also staying in the inn. Gilman broke up the fight, threw the assailants out, and told the others to go up to bed. Their hearts still racing, the men went upstairs to the room they shared.

Their terror was only beginning. Later that evening a band of "Indians" appeared out of the night and burst in upon Dunbar's men as they settled in to sleep. About "Thirty" men stormed the room, cried "now you Doggs we have got you and will be the Death of you,"[24] and extinguished the candles. Then they grabbed the surveyor general's crew from their beds, dragging them out of their bed chamber and to the head of the stairs. The assailants pulled Pitman, Gallaway, and the others down the whole flight, "Tumbled us down headlong,"[25] until they reached the door to the inn.

Once outside, the men were beaten with clubs. Pitman himself was pummeled so badly he was in "Great Danger of his Life having Received Several wounds" and lost "a Great Deal of Blood."[26] He regained his legs enough to flee and was tracked into the night by a man who told him "he would be the Death of him." Pitman desperately ran to a neighboring house, where he was taken in by a Henry Marshall, who later faced down the mob and denied harboring any of Dunbar's men, at which point the group threatened the Exeter resident with "disguised voices" and proceeded to circle the house for hours to the "Great Terrour" of the occupants.[27]

When Gallaway was hauled out of the inn, he said he heard his captors debating whether to "beat" or "murther" him; they decided to let him go to tell his boss that the same would happen to him if he came back. As he ran into the dark they pelted him with stones. Two more of Dunbar's men, William Stiggins and William Starrat, were hurried out of the building by a concerned woman who said, "Lord help us I am afraid their will be Murther,"[28] and they were able to blend in with the crowd gathered around the tavern and escape. Another of Dunbar's men, Walter Olsten, was walking back to the inn from the boat, unaware of what happened, when a bunch of men in disguise jumped him and beat him savagely. And Joseph Miller was hauled to the edge of the riverbank and thrown down fifteen feet over a pile of boards, hurting his back. He lay there all night not daring to be seen again.

The next day the surveyor's men regrouped and returned to their boat to leave. They found it "cut to pieces."[29] Dunbar later tried to get local town officials to accompany the local sheriff to investigate Copyhold Mill, Black Rock Mill, Upper and Lower Tuckaway Mills, Wadly Mill, Book Mill, Gilman's Mill, and Piscassack Mill. They were then to hire carriages, confiscate the boards, and ship them to Dunbar. The surveyor general received a letter dated August 21 in return. It read: "We received your honour's Letter of 7r 27 'wherein you require Some of us to go with [the Sheriff] . . . to Certaine Mills in this Town'. . . but we have not yet complied with your other Demands, Nor can we find upon the Most Deliberate consideration any authority to Support us in So doing."[30]

From his home in New Hampshire, Dunbar simply sat and stewed. He came to consider the work of Surveyor General as practically impossible to carry out under the circumstances, and always saw himself as the innocent. In a report home, he wrote: "I have no view but to discharge my duty which must occasion Murmurings and Complaints from ungovernable people who would be under no Control and who will never behaave as English Subjects until this Country is under another form of Government."[31]

The hated surveyor general wasn't wrong. Anti-crown sentiment was beginning to fester all around him. The people of the colonies were growing increasingly discontent with their lot, from the woods of Maine and New Hampshire to the legal chambers of Boston and Philadelphia. The mob attack on the surveyor general's men would come to be called the Mast Tree Riot, and it showed for the first time the depth of anger felt by colonists. Among the first acts of political violence directed at the king's representatives—and policies—it inspired the events that followed thirty-eight years later up the road in Weare, New Hampshire, which in turn gave ideas to certain men in Boston who were incensed about taxes on tea.

Pl. 145

Bessa del.

Audouël sc.

While Pine.
Pinus Strobus.

The white pine, *Pinus strobus*.

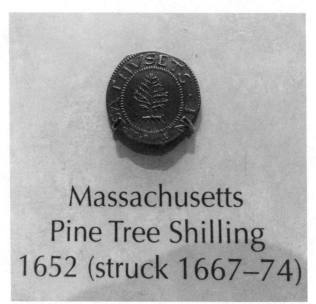

Massachusetts
Pine Tree Shilling
1652 (struck 1667–74)

The colonists created their own currency in 1652, with a shilling depicting the pine tree. The king was outraged by this display of independence—only the crown could mint money. The designer of the coin was a devout Puritan and thought the image of the king was an affront to God, so he substituted an icon of New England. The pine tree became a symbol of independence.

Surveyor teams marking trees with the hated king's broad arrow.

The flag of New England. Colonists replaced St. George's cross in the canton with an image they felt better represented their new home and spirit of independence—a pine tree.

Historians still debate whether the flag of New England actually flew at the Battle of Bunker Hill, but it appears in the most famous depiction of the event by American painter John Trumbull, flying above colonial forces as General Joseph Warren bleeds out on the ground.

AN APPEAL TO HEAVEN

The eastern white pine was prominently displayed on the six ships commissioned by George Washington in October 1775. George Washington's aide Colonel Joseph Reed came up with the design of the "Appeal to Heaven" flag, writing to Colonel Glover on October 20, 1775, "What do you think of a flag with a white ground, a tree in the middle, the motto 'Appeal to Heaven?'"

Naval ensign of Massachusetts. Putting pine trees on naval flags became a tradition in New England.

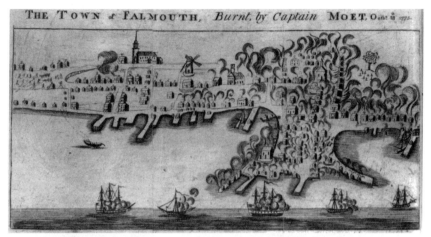

When Maine colonists blocked the way of mast agent Thomas Coulson, and arrested British officer Henry Mowatt (or Moet), the English burned the town of Falmouth to the ground in 1775. Mentioned in the Declaration of Independence, the event stunned the colonies and rallied to the rebel cause many who were still loyal to the king.

Hated surveyor of the king's woods, David Dunbar built his own little empire based on pine trees.

Towering and majestic, often straight and with few low branches, *Pinus strobus* was perfect for making masts.

Province of
New-Hampſhire.}

By the SURVEYOR-GENERAL *of the*
KING's *Woods in* NORTH-AMERICA, *&c. &c.*

WHEREAS ſome Perſons have
formerly gone into the KING's
Woods, and thence hauled White
Pine Logs into *Connecticut* River,
without Licence, and againſt the
Laws made and provided for the
Preſervation of the KING's Woods;
which Timber has been ſold to
others, who have purchaſed, not
knowing it was unlawful, & there-
by expoſed themſelves to the Penal-
ties of the Law :

THEREFORE, to prevent ſuch
fraudulent Practices, and to pre-
ſerve the Innocent from the Evil,
and unjuſtifiable Impoſitions of
others,---NOTICE is hereby given,
That all White Pine Logs cut and
hauled out of the King's Woods
into *Connecticut* River, or elſewhere,
will be ſeized to his MAJESTY's
Uſe, and Treſpaſſers dealt with according to Law.

Portſmouth, 1ſt *January,* 1770.

A broadside from the king published in Portsmouth, January 1770. Source: Library of Congress.

Because of their unwieldy size, pine masts were difficult to transport and required special ships, often with the ability to load from the stern. S. F. Manning illustration.

Pines could be massive. Note the size of the ax.

CHAPTER EIGHT

Tree of Liberty, City of Fire

*A more wanton, indefensible assault upon an undefended city
has not disgraced the annals of modern warfare.*
—THOMAS B. REED, PORTLAND, MAINE, 1886[1]

ON THE 8TH OF APRIL, 1775, JOHN HANCOCK AND SAMUEL
Adams fled Boston to hide out in Lexington—they knew the
British were coming for them. Loyalists and English spies had
alerted General Thomas Gage that the rebel colonists were stock-
piling munitions twenty miles from Boston, and the British were
busy crafting plans to capture them. Tensions had been high and
emotions in ferment ever since March 6, when the city marked
the anniversary of what was being called the Boston Massacre.

The fervor was felt even on the distant coast of Maine, where
Colonel Samuel Thompson of the Brunswick militia received a
letter from the Provincial Congress dated April 11. His orders
were clear: stop the loyalist mast agent Edward Parry from shipping white pine spars to the British at Nova Scotia. No one in the
Provincial Congress wanted the British navy to grow any stronger
than it already was. Thompson's task was essentially the same
thing the English had tried to do in Concord: prevent the enemy
from accessing the tools it needed to wage war.

A tavern owner from the small town of Brunswick, Province of Maine, Colonel Thompson was eager to show his support for the patriot cause. He was overweight, always outspoken—though he had a speech impediment—and never had the benefit of a formal education, but was quick of wit and much admired in the village on Casco Bay. Even at the age of forty, his mouth tended to get him into trouble, but it didn't stop him from being elected to the board of selectmen in his hometown three times and given control of the local militia just the year before. His friends liked to tell the story of the interchange he had with a lawyer from the general court, who noticed Thompson couldn't read. "If your education had been good you would have been a great man," the barrister said to Thompson, who replied: "his face radiant with fun and hope, 'If I had your education, I could put you in my pocket.'"[2]

Six months before he received his letter from the continental congress, Colonel Thompson had been part of a delegation from Maine that traveled to Boston to share with the famous British leader General Gage "the disturbed condition of the province."[3] Shortly after that, he was named to a committee responsible for finding the names of people who had accepted appointments from Parliament—in other words, for outing loyalists and then publishing their names.

The letter from the Provincial Congress that April gave Colonel Thompson yet another mission, instructing him, in very clear language, to search the coastal communities of Brunswick, Woolwich, and Georgetown and put a stop to "one Mr. Perry" who was "endeavoring to supply our enemies with masts, spars and timber." Thompson was to "make use of all proper and effective measures to prevent their aiding him in procuring such articles."[4]

Edward Parry, the second son of a wealthy English family, was a civilian employee of the Royal Navy, responsible for securing the all-important white pine masts for His Majesty's ships, the same role held by Westbrook, Waldo, and Gulston before him. Based in

Portsmouth, he did most of his work in New Hampshire and the Province of Maine, traveling to docks and arranging shipments to "His Majesty's dock yard" in Halifax.

Several days after receiving the letter, Colonel Thompson and a company of twenty militia found Edward Parry and his crew of mastwrights in Georgetown readying two hundred white pine spars for shipment to the Royal Navy, and they seized him and another loyalist, John Bernard, taking them into custody with "great violence," as Parry would later write. Parry immediately appealed to Boston for help.

A committee was appointed to look into his case, and its verdict reflected the prevailing patriot sentiment in Boston. They ruled "considering his close connection and dependance on persons employed by the Crown—his disposition to supply our enemies with Masts, Plank & contrary to the known sentiments of this people"—and recommended he be transferred to "some inland Town which shall be more than seventy miles distant from all the seaports in this Colony, there to be detained." Which is essentially what happened—he was taken to Sturbridge, Massachusetts, and placed under house arrest (albeit only sixty-some miles from the coast at Boston).

After taking the masts from Parry into custody, Colonel Thompson reported back to the Provincial Congress in his version of the king's tongue:

> [I] am about to move about two hundred of white pine masts and other Stuff got for our Enemies' use. Sir, having heard of the Cruill murders they have don in our Province, makes us more Resolute than ever, and finding that the Sword is drawn first on their side, that we shall be animated with that noble Spirit that wise men ought to be, until our Just Rights and Libertys are Secured to us. Sir, my heart is with every true Son of America, though my Person can be in but one place at once, tho very soon hope to be with you on the spot.[5]

In other words, he couldn't believe the British committed homicide at Lexington and Concord, and he was ready to travel south if need be.

The controversial masts sat in Georgetown for three weeks before the next Provincial Congress was held in Watertown to determine what to do with them. A motion was made "That some measures might be taken to preserve a Number of large Masts, Plank &c now lying in Kennebeck River, and to prevent their being carried to Hallifax where they must be appropriated to the Injury of this Country."[6] The motion was resolved, but another seven weeks passed before anyone thought to do something with the masts.

At the end of June, the Provincial Congress ordered Colonel Thompson to return to Georgetown and "get assistance and remove said Masts and other Timber to a place of Safty The Costs not Exceeding forty pound . . . as it appears Said Edward Parry is not Friendly to this Country."[7] The masts would sit for months before this was accomplished—things got a little heated for Colonel Samuel Thompson. The saga that would later be called Thompson's War was only just beginning.

While he was being detained in Sturbridge, Edward Parry wrote to Henry Mowatt, the British commander of His Majesty's ship *Canceaux*, which was anchored in Falmouth harbor. (Portland was called Falmouth until 1785.) Commissioned as a lieutenant in 1758, Mowatt had taken control of the *Canceaux* in 1764 and quickly found himself actively involved in the mast business, protecting the king's interests. In 1772, he loaned John Wentworth a vessel to explore reported violations along the Maine coast. Wentworth indeed found "about 200 tons of timber and 70 thousand feet of Deals cut from the King's woods." This wasn't a major haul, but Wentworth and Mowatt were pleased because it sent a message, "restraining Trespasses as people find their Remote Situation does not save them."[8]

In 1775 Mowatt had been in Maine on yet more mast business, protecting another English mast agent, Thomas Coulson. Eager Falmouth patriots had prevented Coulson from unloading a shipment of rigging for a mast ship he was having built at a local shipyard, calling it a violation of the Continental Congress's Articles of Association, which did not allow importation from England. They also refused to let him take the masts that his crews had cut. Angered, Coulson had written to the admiralty in Boston for help, and Mowatt was dispatched aboard the sixteen-gun sloop *Canceaux* to see to it that the mast agent could conduct his all-important business. Falmouth had become the biggest mast shipping port in the colonies, and the British were all too aware how much they needed these spars.

Parry's note, by contrast with Coulson's plea for help, was simply to apprise Lieutenant Mowatt of his situation, and inform him that due to the "unfortunate Temper of the Times," he would be unable to fulfill his mast order with the Halifax yard. Doing so, he wrote, would be "extremely hazardous for some time to attempt it unless affairs take a Sudden Turn." The letter was all straightforward business until the end, where Parry scribbled a portentous post script: "There are some Reports spread here of an attempt to Surprize the *Canceaux*."

The colonel was indeed planning an attack on Mowatt's ship, incensed by the fact that the British had the temerity to sail to Falmouth with a vessel of war only weeks after fighting began at Lexington and Concord. In fact, it seems his plan was not much of a secret. The Provincial Congress was tipped off about Thompson from someone else in Georgetown and sent official word to the colonel to "desist from such an attempt."[9]

For a while, Thompson appeared to acquiesce, but then there he was, ahead of about fifty men, many of whom had their blood pumping from the capture of Edward Parry, cruising up the coast to Falmouth from Brunswick and landing at Back Cove just behind Falmouth Neck. The militiamen each had a sprig of the white pine's cousin, the spruce, in their hats; they used a spruce tree, stripped of its lower branches, as their standard. Thus adorned, they camped secretly in the woods for several hours—before the captain of the hated British warship fell right into their hands.

Captain Henry Mowatt was out for a leisurely evening stroll along with his ship's surgeon and a local minister when he stumbled upon Thompson and his men. The Brunswick colonel seized the British officer and took him to Marston's Tavern, an alehouse located in what was then the center of Falmouth. The hip-roofed building was one of three popular gathering places for patriots (the others were Alice Greele's and John Greenwood's), and Thompson and his militia held their prize there while they had a few drinks and decided what to do with him. The Brunswick men met with the Falmouth militia at the tavern, and they voted to hold Mowatt and proceed straight to the bay to sink the *Canceaux*. The citizens of Falmouth, however, were terrified of the repercussions of such an act. And there were many among them, just as there were in communities throughout the colonies, who remained loyal to the king. While Maine was a hotbed of rebel sentiment—thanks to years of frustration with the White Pine Acts and mistreatment from English officials like Surveyor of the Woods David Dunbar—many of the affluent merchants of the growing community of Falmouth had financial ties to England. The province was divided along economic and geographical lines—the farther from southern Maine and the coast, the more likely to be opposed to the crown.

The Loyalists in the tavern that evening urged Thompson to let the British captain go. Their stores, they argued, were not sufficient to withstand an English blockade of the community. Their arguments were bolstered by Mowatt's second in command, an officer named Lieutenant Hogg. When he heard what happened, Hogg issued Colonel Thompson an ultimatum: release Mowatt within two hours or the city will be reduced to ashes. Thompson's zeal came through in his answer: "F— f— fire away. For every gun you fire I will cut off a joint of Mowatt."[10] Two guns were eventually fired as warning, but they contained no shot and did no damage other than terrifying residents of Falmouth Neck. Mowatt kept his joints. The shots were enough, though, to cause companies of colonial soldiers from Gorham, Cape Elizabeth, Stroudwater, and Scarborough to move to the scene.

At nine that evening, Colonel Thompson relented to pressure from the affluent citizens of Falmouth Neck and naively let Mowatt return to his ship, on the promise that he would turn himself in the next morning. Two officers, General Jedidiah Preble and Colonel Freeman, even said they'd stand in for Mowatt should he not return.

Of course, Mowatt never did return, "fearing for his own life," and Thompson and his men were incensed. Their rage grew even further when they asked for payment for their services from the wealthy Tories of Falmouth Neck and were all but laughed at. So they took out their anger on the property of Thomas Coulson, whose mast ship had caused the problem to begin with. They dragged off one of Coulson's boats and another vessel belonging to Mowatt and hauled them for safekeeping to Back Cove. An overly eager patriot, Calvin Lombard, of Gorham, even marched down to the waterfront and fired two shots at the *Canceaux*, which lodged themselves in her side.

From the safety of his ship, Mowatt demanded that Lombard be given up, Coulson's property returned, and the good townspeople dispel "the mob from the country," or he would bomb the town. The Tories of Falmouth were able to placate him, and Mowatt eventually weighed anchor and sailed for Portsmouth with Coulson.

At the end of the tense affair, General Jedidiah Preble wrote: "Mowatt never will fire upon the town in any case whatever."[11]

Mowatt would prove him wrong yet again.

That summer was filled with tense moments, and the controversial mast agent Coulson was responsible for some of them. He returned to Falmouth in June to claim his masts, but found that they had been hidden away by colonists. He demanded their return, but the people declared him an enemy of the country and refused. Later that month another of Coulson's boats cruised the Piscataqua in search of white pine spars, but it was intercepted by "five men and three guns" and seized. Coulson's men were let go but their vessel was impounded. Once again, the British agent turned tail, sailing back to Boston.

In Boston, a man from Maine happened to talk to Admiral Graves, who told him that if the men of Falmouth did not allow Coulson to load his masts, he would "send a ship or ships and beat the town down about their ears."[12]

Four months later, Henry Mowatt sailed back into Falmouth harbor with a flotilla of five warships—the sixteen-gun *Canceaux*, the twenty-gun *Cat*, the twelve-gun schooner HMS *Halifax*, the bomb sloop HMS *Spitfire*, and a supply ship, the HMS *Symmetry*. The fleet anchored in the harbor, just out of range of the city's defenses. The sight of the British vessels filled residents with fear, especially in light of what had happened during the summer in Boston, at the Battle of Bunker Hill. East of Falmouth, a ragtag group of rebels had boarded and seized an English warship in Machias in June, tipping off the first naval battle of the burgeoning conflict. In Falmouth, they naturally assumed the war had finally come to them. Some residents were said to have been relieved when they found out that Captain Mowatt was in command, assuming he would remember how many of the good citizens of Falmouth had argued for his release.

Little did they know that Falmouth, along with Machias, was already on a list of target cities drawn up by the British Admiralty. For a variety of reasons, the communities of Salem, Marblehead,

Gloucester, Ipswich, Newburyport, Portsmouth, Saco, and the two other Maine ports were to be "chastised" with punitive strikes. Thompson and his men had seized a British officer—and they were to be punished. Vice Admiral Samuel Graves instructed Captain Mowatt to "carry on such Operations upon the Sea Coasts . . . as you shall judge most effective for suppressing . . . the Rebellion . . . to lay waste burn and destroy such Sea Port towns as are accessible to His Majesty's ships."[13]

Henry Mowatt was all too willing to carry out the order.

On October 17 Mowatt showed his form of mercy to the people of Falmouth, sending an officer ashore with a letter in hand. In it the captain gave townspeople two hours to evacuate before he firebombed the city. "After so many premeditated attacks on the legal prerogative of the best of sovereigns," he wrote, "after the repeated instances you have experienced in Britain's long forbearance of the rod of correction, and the manifest and paternal extention of her hands to embrace again and again, have been regarded as vain . . . you have been guilty of the most unpardonable rebellion."[14]

Mowatt continued that the people of Falmouth would suffer a "just punishment" for their actions, and he gave them two hours to "remove without delay, the human specie out of the said town,"[15] after which he would hoist a red flag up the mast of the *Canceaux* to signal that bombardment was about to begin. Any townspeople willing to bow to the king were welcome to visit his ship and put themselves under his protection.

A group of Falmouth's prominent citizens met with Mowatt under these pretenses. The lieutenant said he would spare the city if residents would pledge allegiance to the king; the small delegation convinced him to hold off on bombardment until 8:00 the next morning to at least give people enough time to gather belongings and leave. In exchange for that reprieve they were willing to hand over weapons, including gun carriages. Mowatt agreed. No one was willing to make his pledge, though, and the people of Falmouth spent the night running about like squirrels trying to save their most prized possessions. Horses pulled carts and carriages all through the night, taking terrified townspeople into the countryside. Women and children left on foot. And companies of colonial militia arrived in town to see if they could help. Aside from a few small arms, no one turned over munitions.

Mowatt hauled up the red flag at 9:40 on the clear morning of October 19, and the first shots exploded the calm. Eight hours of constant firebombing followed. "The four British ships poured a horrible shower of balls, bombs, carcasses, live shells, grapeshot and musket balls from their howitzers, mortars and cannon. Carcasses, large iron balls filled with oil and flammable material, were ignited by the cannon blast." More than three thousand rounds rained down on the town, but the poor ammunition, winds, and a determined brigade of citizens kept the town from being consumed by flame. Outraged, Captain Mowatt sent British marines ashore. They landed around 3:00 in the afternoon and set fire to many buildings by throwing torches through windows. Colonial militiamen engaged the landing party but soon ran out of gunpowder.

By early evening, the town of Falmouth was finally burning. "The crackling of the flames, the falling of the houses, the bursting of the shells, the heavy thunder of the cannon threw the elements into frightful noise and commotion," wrote local reverend Jacob Bailey. "Now lengthening pyramids of fire ascended horribly bright from the dissolving structures and the inhabitations of pride, vanity, and affluence crumbled to ashes, while their late possessors beheld the shocking appearance with a mixture of astonishment and humble indignation."[16]

When the sun went down and Mowatt's ships weighed anchor, Falmouth was decimated. More than three hundred houses and hundreds of businesses and industrial buildings were destroyed, and the captain sank several ships in the harbor. More than a third of Falmouth's estimated population of twenty-five hundred faced the prospect of spending the winter homeless. Thankfully, the only casualties reported were among the British marines, two of whom were "slightly wounded" upon landing.

Mowatt wrote back to his superiors that he had carried out his orders, seeing to it that, "notwithstanding the vast numbers of armed men," who had congregated in town, Falmouth was "laid into ashes."[17]

Chapter Nine

Revolution Comes

Who leaves the pine-tree, leaves his friend, Unnerves his strength, invites his end.

—Ralph Waldo Emerson

The firebombing of Falmouth stunned the colonies. The burning of a town of innocents made for ideal propaganda, and news of it spread quickly, featured in newspapers up and down the east coast. Many colonists who, even after hostilities broke out at Lexington and Concord, refused to give up on the goodness of the English crown, had their minds changed instantly. Despite the lack of blood, it was ugly business, putting residents of a northern colony out into the streets as winter approached. Even the French were horrified, their foreign secretary writing his support of the colonies: "I can hardly believe this absurd as well as barbaric procedure on the part of an enlightened and civilized nation."[1]

George Washington, named commander in chief a few months earlier in June, called Mowatt's aggression proof that the British were planning "the most cruel and savage war that ever a civilized nation engaged in."[2] And the colonies took steps to make sure it wouldn't happen again. The bombardment prompted the Second Continental Congress to create a fleet to protect the coast, an act that John Adams referred to as the "true origin of the American navy."[3]

After the event, each colony was encouraged by the Continental Congress to declare itself as self-governing, completely independent of British rule, months before the formal decree would be made in July 1776, when the Declaration of Independence was drafted. Included in the famed document was a reference to the attack on Falmouth, among many other grievances, stating that the king "has plundered our seas, ravaged our coasts, burnt our towns and destroyed the lives of our people."[4]

Through the burning of the Casco Bay community, the British turned the people of northern New England so firmly against them that they cut themselves off to the very mast supply they would need to wage war. Perhaps the greatest irony of the event was that it began with a mast surplus—the supply that British mast agent Coulson wanted to load—and ended with a mast shortage for the British. Lumbermen across northern New England put down their axes and took up muskets, mustering for war.

The white pine helped precipitate the conflict and became a symbol of grievances felt by colonists. It continued to have a role as the war played out, as a galvanizing icon and as an all-important component of waterborne combat. Ships needed flags, troops needed uniforms—the colonists found a perfect bit of iconography in the pine tree. It was instantly recognizable. It was simple to draw. It represented their short history as a new American entity: The historic seal of the Massachusetts Bay colony depicted a native standing between two trees, one of which is a pine, and the pine tree shilling, so controversial when it was first minted, later banned by the king, was also a likely reference point. Ships originating in New England had flown flags bearing the white pine since at least the 1680s. The tree, and the history of contention it represented, was an example of real division between themselves and the king.

Legend has it that the colonists carried a pine flag at the first major battle of the war, what would come to be known as Bunker Hill, in June 1775. History can't confirm or deny whether the simple red standard, with a green pine in the canton, was actually flying atop Breed's Hill, as the colonists fought their first pitched campaign against the British, but it's depicted in the most famous painting of the event, the *Death of General Warren at the Battle of Bunker's Hill June 17, 1775*, by John Trumbull. As the two sides fight in the smoky gloom, the flag is shown above the head of the slumping colonial doctor. After that historic clash, the Continental Army began to surround Boston, and out in the Charles River were gun emplacements set upon barges. Flapping in the breeze above them was yet another pine tree flag, showing *Pinus strobus* beneath the phrase "An Appeal to Heaven" in a bold black font across the top of the banner.

The phrase was one used popularly around the colonies in the years before the war, referencing John Locke's Second Treatise on Government, and calling on God to protect them from the agents of the king. Famed Doctor Joseph Warren, a colonial agitator, Son of Liberty, president of the Massachusetts Provincial Congress, and the dying general in Trumbull's iconic painting, used it in April 1775 when writing a letter to the people of England, shaming the British government for the events of Lexington and Concord: "We will not tamely submit; appealing to Heaven for the justice of our cause, 'we determine to die, or be free.'"[5]

In October 1775, George Washington commissioned seven warships from colonial shipyards. His troops ringed Boston by land, and he wanted to be able to blockade from the sea as well; because Congress was loath to offend England by founding a navy, he paid for the vessels himself. Later that year, Joseph Reed, a Washington aide, wrote to Colonel John Glover about supplies for the Continental Army. He referenced the destruction of Falmouth Neck and offered some heraldry ideas:

We have accounts that the small squadron which sailed some time ago is bombarding Fulmouth and Portsmouth. Our vessels must be careful how they fall in with them. Please to fix upon some particular colour for a flag, and a signal by which our vessels may know one another. What do you think of a flag with a white ground, a tree in the middle, the motto 'Appeal to Heaven?' This is the flag of our floating batteries.[6]

Washington liked the idea, and the flag went to war. The new ensign also impressed the Massachusetts Provincial Congress—so much they made it the naval flag of the state six months later in July 1776, when it began outfitting its own armada to protect its coast from the British. "Resolved, that the uniform of the officers be green and white, and that the colors be a white flag, with a green pine tree, and the inscription, 'An Appeal to Heaven.'"[7] The floating fighting force of Massachusetts was eventually merged with the U.S. Navy.

The sight of a pine tree replacing the St. George cross atop colonial ships may well have rankled the British, but they were probably more bothered by the pine masts to which they were affixed. Symbolism aside, there was the very real fact that the Royal Navy's supply of masts was cut off.

As fighting was breaking out in places like Lexington and Concord, the last shipment of New England masts made its way across the Atlantic, reaching English shores on July 31, 1775, shortly after the news of the Battle of Bunker Hill. The mast ships tended to sail twice a year, once in the spring and later in the season, and during the broad arrow era they carried more than forty-five hundred of New England's finest boles to England for use by the Royal Navy. They would sail no more.

All along the coast colonists were carrying out the directive of the Provincial Congress, keeping the king's agents from claiming any more timbers. Just like the men of Falmouth and Colonel

Thompson in Georgetown, Maine, they were preventing their enemy from availing himself of the tools of war.

Up and down the eastern seaboard, angry colonists waded into mast pools and dragged the long spars off to be hidden away where the king's men couldn't find them (fifty years after Coulson's masts were taken from him in Portland they still sat rotting in the Forest City's harbor). Or they were simply destroyed. Spars and naval stores were burned on Noddle Island in Boston Harbor. Masts were seized in Portsmouth. Halifax readied itself for a raid on the king's yard,[8] a likely target.

On May 17, British captain Andrew Barkley of the HMS *Scarborough* attempted to intervene in Portsmouth on behalf of a Royal Navy mast agent. Just like in Falmouth, locals refused to allow the king's man to take his masts. Barkley apprised Admiral Graves of the situation on May 19:

> *Yesterday, Governor Wentworth sent me a message by his Secretary acquainting me there was about three hundred Men had assembled to carry away a Quantity of Masts, that were in a Pond near the Town. I asked the Secretary if the Governor desired that I might send my Boats to prevent their so doing, he said no, by no means, for if such a thing was attempted they would immediately be cut to pieces.*[9]

The Redcoat captain then asked the governor's secretary what the men intended to do with the pines, and he was told they would move them upriver "for their better Security." Barkley was astonished. "I asked him where they could be so well secured or safe as under the Protection of a King's ship." Wentworth then contacted the captain directly, telling him to stand down, writing, "by which you may see, that they intend they never shall be made use of for the King or his Service."

The British had to simply make do, returning hat in hand to the Baltics looking for replacements. The Royal Navy had become dependent upon the tall straight pines of New England, and yet they had to go back to binding together composite masts out of the Riga firs. The Loyalists of Canada were another option, and the British began buying masts from New Brunswick, Halifax, and the St. John region of what is now Maine. And they suffered for it, finding it difficult to outfit their ships of war. By 1778, the British mast situation was growing dire—"dangerous," as one historian put it. Their supply was at its lowest point in one hundred years.

Meanwhile colonial shipyards were quickly turning out vessels for the war effort. Congress ordered the construction of thirteen frigates to fill out the navy it had cobbled from private vessels and commandeered ships. A year later, General Benedict Arnold hastily built more than a dozen more on Lake Champlain, using timbers felled from the forests of New York.

Mast cutting continued in the woodlands of northern New England, but instead of supplying England, the colonists shipped masts to their allies the French, a slap in the face to King George III. Normally, the Royal Navy would have simply intercepted these valuable timbers but their crippled navy simply wasn't up to the task. Or they lacked the courage, as was the case when the British sloop of war *Rainbow* sailed up the Sheepscot River in Maine, happening upon a ship and a brig loading masts and lumber at the dock in Wiscasset, readying to sail for France. The British captain, Sir George Collyer, seized the vessels. The local militia colonel demanded they be released and, when Collyer refused, the rebel gave the redcoat an ultimatum—let the ship and the brig go on their way and leave the harbor by a specified time or face a cannonade from Daggett's Castle, a high bluff four miles south of the harbor. Since this was his only way out, Collyer relented, and the two ships sailed for France, where the colonists traded the masts for armaments.[10]

It wasn't just naval stores getting through the British Navy's guard. British intelligence learned that the French commander Comte D'Estaing was planning to cross the Atlantic with four thousand troops aboard a dozen ships—reinforcements that would be a huge boon to the Americans in their battle with General Howe. But the English were all but powerless to stop them. The Royal Navy's vessels were in poor repair and suffering from a "serious lack of masts and supplies," and they had to protect their own shores from the threat of the French.

The Royal Navy scraped together what vessels it could spare—thirteen ships of the line—and Admiral John Byron, the Romantic poet Lord Byron's grandfather, set off in hot pursuit of the French troop transports on June 9, 1778. The French fleet had sailed from Toulon on April 15, making the task of catching them almost impossible—but they had spent about a month in the Mediterranean, and Byron figured he could intercept them at Gibraltar and send them to the bottom.

The admiral crashed into a squall on July 3, however, having only made it a third of the way across the Atlantic. The pummeling southwest gale was worse than a bombardment. In the high winds, the old dry masts of his fleet, sapped of their elasticity by decades in the sun, snapped one after another. Ship carpenters did their best to bind the spars back together but they were weak and came plummeting back down to the decks. The English fleet was blown apart by the storm, and Byron ordered it to turn and head back for England. A handful of ships crept on toward America, unaware of the admiral's orders.

One such ship was the ironically named *Invincible*, helmed by a Captain Evans. On August 13, on its way to North America, the ship encountered more weather and the captain had the men fell the mainmast like a pine in a forest to prevent it from collapsing. No sooner was this done than the "foremast went in three pieces, all of which fell on the forecastle and wounded several men but only one killed."[11] Evans was able to keep the vessel moving and finally made it to Halifax—but only after encountering D'Estaing's fleet and barely escaping.

The French troops made it to America, and the only aid that Admiral Byron—often referred to as "Foul-Weather Jack" by his sailors—was able to provide General Howe was a single seventy-four-gun ship.

Thanks to masts from America, the French navy would continue to be a formidable opponent to the English. At the end of the war, when the Royal Navy attempted to send a fleet carrying seven thousand reinforcements to help General Cornwallis, who was doing battle with Washington and the Marquis de Lafayette at Yorktown, Virginia, they met a cannonade from French warships that snapped their masts. With the extreme shortage of masts, the Brits were forced to limp back to New York to find replacements.

With new masts in place, the English armada got back under way on October 19, 1781, when Admiral Thomas Graves sailed with twenty-three ships in a race to aid Cornwallis. They were too late, Cornwallis was surrounded. The French and colonial regulars overran British positions and the English capitulated to George Washington.

Finding and installing the new masts had taken too long—the war was over.

Years later, historians would speculate what the outcome of the war might have been if a powerful, well-outfitted Royal Navy had been able to set up a blockade and prevent the French from coming to the aid of the Americans, forcing the Yanks to do battle on their own.

And a British naval officer, too, lamented what might have been. In 1788 he wrote: "Indeed, it appeared as if the elements had joined our foes, for storms and hurricanes assisted them to destroy our navy, which by their own strength they were unable to shake."[12]

Storms, hurricanes—and pines.

Chapter Ten

The Aroostook War

The forests are the flags of Nature. They appeal to all and awaken inspiring universal feelings. Enter the forest and the boundaries of nations are forgotten. It may be that sometime an immortal pine will be the flag of a united and peaceful world.
—Enos Mills

In the cold winter of February 1839, Rufus McIntire and his men hiked through the forest along the Aroostook River, a region that put the north in the North Woods, 130 miles from Bangor and as remote as remote got in the new state of Maine. At the head of a company of two hundred, McIntire wound his way through the trees down to the river, the men behind him holding rifles in one hand and parting branches with the other. McIntire, a Bangor land agent, was in charge of the militia, but he'd asked for the help of Hastings Strickland, a businessman from the city on the Penobscot. Strickland was building an empire in pine trees, riding a timber-cutting boom that had turned the Queen City into the Lumber Capital of the World in the first decades of the nineteenth century. Strickland was also sheriff of Penobscot County, and it was in that capacity that he'd been invited along by McIntire. The sheriff had assembled the small armed force, and they moved at his orders.

Though the woods were heavy with winter and quiet, stealth with a posse of this size was all but impossible, and plenty of locals saw them coming anyway. The chill in the air was due to more than the famously frigid February temperatures of Aroostook County—locals from the nearby village were hostile to the militia, and the tension was almost palpable. Anger and frustration had been mounting in this part of the country for months—years even—and all at once things were beginning to spiral beyond the control of authorities.

McIntire, Strickland, and their men reached the edge of the Aroostook River, near the upcountry hamlet of Masardis, and put the run to several lumber crews who were felling big pines and dragging them to the river to be pushed in for the spring run. The posse forced the timber cutters to flee into the woods or risk arrest. In the flurry of their departure, some lumbermen were caught and detained. After making their way through the lumber camps along the river, McIntire left Strickland and his men and went to a nearby farm to speak with residents of the area, who were outraged to see a group of armed men marching through their community. McIntire intended to wait there for a New Brunswick warden, who was traveling along the Upper St. John River and would be returning to the region soon.

Nothing went as planned, however.

At about midnight on February 12, McIntire found himself surrounded by a group of rifle-toting men, captured, and taken as a prisoner to the Canadian town of Fredericton. Strickland heard of the arrest, and he was also given the impression that an armed force of three hundred Canadians was heading his way. He had his men fall back with all haste to a defensible position near the Aroostook, and they dug in to wait for the inevitable battle.

It looked like war would follow.

Fifty volunteers marched north from Augusta to join Strickland's band and to defend American sovereignty. They were followed by thousands more. Within two weeks of the arrest of McIntire, Maine governor John Fairfield had moved 1,000 troops to the Aroostook River. He then asked the legislature for 10,343 more, and was granted them—they were ordered to the region with the "arms and equipment complete for active service." They were to report "with the least possible delay"[1] for a tour of duty that would initially be three months, and $800,000 was approved for expenses. The 2nd and 3rd Divisions of the Maine militia assembled and began to make their way north to add their numbers to the troops already sent. Eventually, a total of forty-six companies of infantry and artillery were called to active duty. The Maine soldiers captured the New Brunswick warden with whom McIntire had been planning to parlay and took him back to Bangor.

None of this did anything to ease the mounting tensions.

The Canadians were outraged, and they, too, began turning the gears of war. New Brunswick's Lieutenant Governor Sir John Harvey denounced the "invasion" of McIntire and Strickland and sent out an appeal for volunteers. He demanded the American troops withdraw from the region along the Aroostook and said that the British government gave him the authority to hold the area by force if necessary. (New Brunswick was then a British colony.) He then ordered two infantry companies to Madawaska, and British regulars were dispatched to join them. Their orders were to reinforce the St. John River, Tobique, and the all-important Temiscouata Portage.

Hearing of the situation along the Maine border, President Martin Van Buren addressed Congress, where he noted the rights of Maine but urged the state to avoid any bloodshed. The next day the Senate Foreign Relations Committee recommended that both Maine and New Brunswick stand down and remove the troops massing in the St. John Valley, but the recommendation was ignored. Instead, Congress passed a bill authorizing President Van Buren to raise more than fifty thousand more troops and provided $10 million for expenses.

Van Buren decided he needed a forceful figure on the American side and sent General Winfield Scott to take control of the situation. Scott was to report only to the president. Known as "Old Fuss and Feathers" to his men, the general had made his name in the War of 1812 and was in national headlines again for shepherding the Cherokee nation along the infamous Trail of Tears. He would go on to become the longest-serving general in American history.

As General Scott traveled to the region, the Maine militia and the Canadians held their positions on either side of the St. John River Valley, staring at each other through gun sights.[2]

A lot was at stake. In the years immediately after the Revolutionary War, when the woods finally seemed safe from natives, French soldiers, and redcoats, the interior regions of New England began to see rapid growth. People steadily flocked inland, looking for land. This was especially true of Maine, then still a woodsy neighborhood of Massachusetts. The state set up an office to issue land grants to veterans, both to help defray the heavy debt of the war and to encourage settlement up north. Lots of 150 acres went for $1 an acre on any river big enough to navigate and on shorefront. Inland lots were free, though the grantee had to clear sixteen acres in four years. Huge swaths of the province were distributed in lotteries, often snapped up by forward-thinking investors.

In 1792, William Bingham, a businessman from Philadelphia, bought himself a small slice of Maine—more than a million acres. Washington's secretary of war, General Henry Knox, put cash down for a massive spread, too, acquiring tens of thousands of acres. His wife was one of the heirs of the famous Waldo patent, and he wanted to move north. Knox built his stately home just a short walk from the spot where George Weymouth came ashore in 1606 in the St. George River hamlet of Thomaston.

In the new nation's first census, done in 1790, this part of Massachusetts had 96,000 residents. In 1820, when Maine was admitted to the union, it had grown to 298,335 hardy souls. And just twenty years later, as troops massed on either side of the St. John, aiming artillery pieces at each other, it had almost doubled, surpassing half a million.

Most of the population of the region still lived below Bangor and along the coast, but demographics were changing, and it was in the sparsely settled northern half of the state, still covered in a thicket of forestlands, that the lumber industry really took off. Relations between the two nations had been repaired, at least enough that the forests of New England shipped masts again to Great Britain in mass quantities—n fact, more masts than ever. The *Journal of the House of Commons* in the United Kingdom reported that the "consumption of timber, for the Navy only . . . Has been more than double, from 1771–1791"[3] to what it had been in the twenty years prior to the war. Nothing a little pine pitch can't patch up.

The Royal Navy's hunger for masts had eaten almost all of the available trees along the rivers of southern Maine, the Piscataqua, and Presumpscot, and Saco. By the end of the war, timber cruisers were moving steadily north in search of pine stands. Lumber camps were set up along the riverways above Bangor—in unorganized North Woods townships—and the great trees were dropped and fed into feeder streams to be driven down to the Queen City for processing.

The lumber industry was almost timeless—a sawyer or a teamster or a driver transplanted from the 1680s on the Piscataqua above Portsmouth would have felt entirely comfortable in the woods above Bangor in the 1820s.

Once a small backwater burgh in the hinterlands, Bangor in a very short time grew into one of the nation's most important cities, riding a wave of pine that floated down the Penobscot. The first sawmill was set up there in 1772, and by 1816 about a million board feet of pine was being processed annually. Sixty years later, the city boasted more than three hundred mills, whining through thirty million board feet a year.

By the 1830s, the city on the Penobscot was considered the Lumber Capital of the World, and the eastern white pine was the tall, pitchy, backbone of the economy. In the decade before the troops of Maine and New Brunswick moved to defend the border, the state of Maine exported $7 million worth of goods— $182 million in today's dollars—and most of it was cut from the woodlands. By 1832, the city had shipped more than two hundred million, and the river was so choked with wood that residents could walk from one shore to the other (roughly eight hundred feet). When war looked imminent on the Aroostook frontier, in 1839, more than ninety million million board feet were felled and processed through Bangor annually and most of it was eastern white pine.

When Thoreau made his famous visit to Bangor in 1846 he was amazed to find that ships were stuck in port for days at a time because they couldn't—or wouldn't—sail through the timbers. They would wait it out, their numbers swelling to as many as three thousand vessels. While the saws turned, the city prospered. Thoreau set the scene in *The Maine Woods*:

> *There stands the city of Bangor, fifty miles up the Penobscot, at the head of navigation for vessels of the largest class, the principal lumber depot on this continent with a population of twelve thousand, like a star on the edge of night, still hewing at the forest of which it is built, already overflowing with the luxuries and refinement of Europe, and sending vessels to Spain, to England and to the West Indies for its groceries.*[4]

Indeed, it was a prosperous place, surprising in its sophistication. One of the nation's great palace hotels, the Bangor House, was built in 1833, as the city's fathers were angling to transform Bangor into a center of northeast shipping that would eclipse Boston to the south. The hotel would eventually welcome Ulysses S. Grant, Howard Taft, Benjamin McKinley, and Theodore Roosevelt among its eminent guests. Lumbermen, meanwhile, drank away their wages in a hard part of town called the Devil's Half Acre, where Madame Fan Jones's brothel, the Skyblue House of Pleasure, became world famous.

Bangor pine was sent across the globe to build homes, from nearby Brewer to Britain to the Bahamas. The trees of northern Maine very literally built New England. In the early days of the new nation, homes were typically timber framed, which is to say they had a heavy interior skeleton built of hewed timbers joined by pegs at the corners with the beams often exposed inside. (After the 1700s, the framing was commonly hidden by plaster or trim.) They were generally made of oak or pine, and a three-story dwelling might require up to thirty-five thousand board feet. Savvy carpenters as early as the days leading up to the Revolution learned how to standardize construction for the popular styles, like center chimney capes or center-entry homes, and began to ship premade framing, an early version of modular housing. In the five years before the war, for example, 147 house frames were exported to the West Indies from Portsmouth, which was then a hub of the lumber industry.

Upon his visit to Bangor, Thoreau wrote: "How far men go for the material of their houses! The inhabitants of the most civilized cities in all ages, send into far, primitive forests, beyond the bounds of their civilization, where the moose and bear and savage dwell, for their pine boards for ordinary use."[5]

Before the colonies achieved independence from England, Aroostook County was a wild fastness with many corners that had been little explored by Europeans. After the war, lumbermen gradually began to delve into its dark forestlands in search of pines, dropping them by the side of the region's two famous rivers—the Allagash and St. John—to be run out to mills for processing. But many of the mills were in Canada.

Both the St. John and Allagash rivers had the unusual distinction of flowing north, which made New Brunswick the logical place to sell timber. And a lot of lumber rode the riffles that way. Some Mainers, however, preferred to keep their business in the United States, and used Telos Cut, a manmade channel, to drive their loads south through Chesuncook Lake to the Penobscot and eventually Bangor.

At first the lumber business in Aroostook was small, due to the remote nature of the region and the small numbers of crews working there. As the pine supply was exhausted in the woods to the south, though, pressure mounted on the region and more and more axes moved north. And the Canadians, who for decades had been crossing the border to work in Maine's lumber camps, dropped down into the St. John River Valley and began to cut the woods there for their own mills.

Suddenly everyone wanted the trees of Aroostook—and everyone claimed them as their own. Just as the colonists at Weare and Exeter and throughout the woodlands of New England saw the trees as their own, regardless of the larger geopolitics, both Mainers and New Brunswickers considered the pines of the St. John their trees. Both sides were righteous in their claims, and each thought lumber crews from across the border were trespassing on sovereign land. Fights broke out, but they were mostly minor fisticuffs and everyone simply kept cutting.

Just like kids arguing over toys, both sides also had an element of justice behind their arguments. The St. John River Valley was part of Maine, and it was also Canadian land—it just depended how one interpreted the language. When the Revolution ended, the border between the nations in that part of the country was never firmly drawn, though it was generally accepted that the St. John flowed for about half its run through British territory. At the close of the next great conflict between the two nations, the War of 1812, the English claimed the whole of the St. John Valley, everything above the 46th parallel, or almost a third of what is now Maine. Some American families, though, lived in the region, and the town of Madawaska even had a representative in the state legislature.

At first none of this mattered much. The few residents who lived in the area considered themselves either Canadian or American largely dependent upon the language they spoke. Many Francophone Acadians made their homes in the valley and thought of themselves as Canadians. Mixed among them were New Englanders who spoke English and flew American flags. Everyone got along fine until the lumber industry exploded and the price for a board foot of pine rose to skyscraping heights.

All of a sudden it mattered very much whether you ate ployes or pork and beans before a day working in the woods. When disputes arose over cutting rights, timber crews looked over their shoulders to their public officials for guidance, to make things right. But neither Americans nor Canadians could definitively back up their claims to the land or provide any legal justification. The language in the Treaty of Ghent, which ended the War of 1812, simply referred to a "height of land" between the rivers that empty into the St. Lawrence and the rivers that flowed into the Atlantic. Where exactly that hillock was, and which rivers drained into what, was open to interpretation. Officials from Maine and New Brunswick haggled over the territory for decades, and the larger U.S. and Canadian governments thought it easier to ignore the whole thing and hope it would resolve itself. The border was never clearly defined.

In June 1837, the Brits upped the ante by arresting an American census official who was in Madawaska counting heads and doling out U.S. revenue. The British thought he was trying to buy the favor of area residents, convincing them in the most American of ways that they were indeed American. A British constable stepped in and hauled the census worker to a local jail, but the sheriff there didn't want anything to do with the situation and let the U.S. citizen go.

Then, New Brunswick's Governor Harvey demanded that the agent be arrested again. He was, and this time was taken to a Frederickton jail. Maine's governor Robert P. Dunlap was incensed and proclaimed that American soil had been invaded by a foreign power. He ordered the Maine militia to muster. The Brits released the census taker again.

All of this brought the boundary issue to the fore, and both nations decided it was past time to settle it for good. But they needed an impartial arbiter, a parent to step in between the kids. They took their case to King William of Holland. The good monarch ruled, in all fairness, to draw the line halfway between the boundaries each country was suggesting. Neither side was happy, but the U.S. government was not keen to fight another war with the British and suggested that Maine go along with King William's proposal, even offering the state a million acres of land to sweeten the deal. But that acreage was in Michigan, and Maine was not at all interested. For decades a stalemate of sorts existed, during which the Maine militia drilled, and General John E. Wool made the rounds of the state's forts to make sure they were ready.

Meanwhile, both sides were issuing cutting permits to the same lands, and lumber crews cut all over the place with impunity. As the pine harvesting intensified, so did the debate over the border. And as the disputes over sovereignty got more heated, so did the cutting. Lumbermen from both nations wanted to get their hands on as much pine as they could before it was cut off to them. At first, enforcement of any sort was virtually nonexistent, but gradually, as arguments between rival crews got more confrontational, local governments started stepping in and arresting the occasional timber team for trespass.

Prosecuting illegal cutters was what brought Rufus McIntire, the land agent from Bangor, Sheriff Strickland, and their posse to the St. John River Valley. McIntire had an official commission from the state of Maine and was fully prepared to execute it. New Brunswick was not going to allow it. Governor Harvey was indignant and threatened military force. The Maine militia and U.S. government seemed fully prepared to meet them on the battlefield. A bloody third fight between the Yanks and the Brits looked imminent—all over a remote corner of the country that most Americans had never heard of and would find an unappealing backwater tangle of dark woods if they ever visited. The only thing it had going for it, in the eyes of most, was pine trees.

In the end, however, no shots were ever fired. General Scott was able to defuse the tensions, and the conflict later known as the Aroostook War, the Pork and Beans War, and the Pine Tree War went into the history books as a war of rhetoric only. Governor Harvey finally cooled off and decided to come to the table, giving his word that his troops would stand down. Governor Fairfield agreed to withdraw his armies. Détente was reached. In order to better administer the region, Maine would form a county in the region as the situation eased, formally calling this northern territory Aroostook County in 1839.

In 1842, the British Ambassador Alexander Baring, the 1st Baron Ashburton was dispatched to Washington to formally settle the boundary. He sat down to talks with Daniel Webster, the famous orator and three-time U.S. secretary of state, and they came to terms. England received a piece of land that allowed New Brunswick to maintain communications with the rest of Canada. The United States got prime shorefront on Lakes Champlain and Superior. The border between Maine and New Brunswick was finally drawn with permanent ink, just as it is known today.

The U.S. Senate ratified the Webster-Ashburton Treaty on August 20, 1842. The U.S. government paid Maine $150,000 for its trouble, and reimbursed the state another $200,000 for the expenses it paid out to defend U.S. soil. The Aroostook War was the last time a state would muster to its own defense; after the standoff, the federal government assumed responsibility for all military matters.

All this happened while the pines continued to fall, one after the other, in the woods along the St. John.

It didn't take long to lay waste to the forest. All that military posturing was for just a few more years of cutting—as the trees fell and acre after acre was cleared, sawyers realized their stock was running out. By the Civil War most of the large pine stands of Maine had fallen. The axes of lumbermen found almost all of the *Pinus strobus* there was to cut, and they turned their attention elsewhere. As Thoreau put it, "The forests are held cheap after the white pine has been culled out. . . ."[6] Many simply stepped over to that close cousin of the pine, the spruce, which outnumbered pines four to one in Maine before anyone started harvesting trees, and began to hew away at it instead. Others looked for pine to cut elsewhere.

Lumbermen from Aroostook and Bangor migrated to New York and Pennsylvania, and eventually pushed on to the mitten of Michigan. By 1870, Michigan had four hundred sawmills working its lower peninsula and it had eclipsed the Pine Tree State for pine production. A year later it was processing more pine boards than the next three states combined. At its peak in 1889–1890, the state cut more than 5.5 billion board feet. Some of its most pine-rich areas, like the High Plains, a sandy region at the top of the mitten, were producing thirty thousand board feet—per acre—and the mills of Saginaw alone produced more than four billion board feet in 1888. According to journalist D. Lawrence Rogers, this was "enough to make a sidewalk of two inch planks, four feet wide, that would reach around the earth almost four times."[7]

Where once beautiful woodlands trundled over hills and along the shores of Lake Michigan, clearcuts blighted the landscape like bad barber jobs. Michigan historians bragged that the trees they took from these barren lands made more millionaires than all the gold in California.[8]

All of this pine was shipped across the Great Lakes and by rail to places like Chicago and Milwaukee, where it was built into homes and businesses. Immigrants not just from New England but from Ireland, Scandinavia, and French Canada all made their way to the Midwest to seek employ in the booming industry. Timber barons grew rich off the hard work of these hardy men and, when the lumbering industry began to fade shortly after the turn of the century, they began to invest their wealth in an exciting new Michigan prospect—automobiles.

Several hundred miles west in Minnesota the trees were dropping, too. Mainers and New Yorkers and Canadians, having exhausted the pine supply in New England and New York, moved to the boundary region. The famous "lob trees," the tallest pines in the woods, used for centuries as landmarks by the region's renowned voyageurs, began to crash to the forest floor. Lumber camps sprouted up like mushrooms after a rain, huge booms swept across lakes, and railroad spurs were threaded into the remotest areas. In the century between 1832 and 1939, Minnesota harvested more than 67.5 billion board feet of eastern white pine, much of it going to build homes in St. Louis and Omaha, Des Moines and Kansas City. Trees were harvested like wheat or corn, whole forests falling to the ax and crosscut saw, as if they were a scourge. By World War II, the idea of making a living in the woods, the traditions of the river driver and the lumberman, became more mythology than reality, fading into the past.

CHAPTER ELEVEN

The Forgotten Forest

I should have liked to come across a large community of pines,
which had never been invaded by the lumbering army.
—HENRY DAVID THOREAU

SOMEHOW IT SEEMS APPROPRIATE THAT TOM SHAFER WAS A
history major. His company pulls Maine's heritage out of Quakish
Lake on a daily basis from May through November. "It's pretty
amazing the stuff you see," says Shafer. "We've pulled out old
barges, all kinds of tools, and a great two-tined anchor." Those
antiques are not what he's after, however. The heritage Shafer and
his business partner, Steve Sanders, look for comes in the form of
old timber, the "forgotten forest," that lies beneath the surface of
the West Branch. Logs cut by river drivers with crosscut saws over
a century ago, boles felled by more modern loggers with chainsaws
and skidders, trunks dropped by fearsome industrial harvesters, all
ended up on the silty bottom of the river, just a few miles from the
mill town of Millinocket.

Quakish Lake is essentially a thousand-acre widening of the
West Branch of the Penobscot, the primary thoroughfare for the
Pine Tree State's famous lumber industry, dropping down from
Moosehead Lake through one of the most densely forested areas
in the northeast, beneath the stony gaze of Mount Katahdin.
Shafer's cranes, working from barges on the lake, haul history up

from twenty feet below the surface, like underwater archeologists, and truck it to facilities on the Golden Road, Maine's logging superhighway, for processing.

"The piles [of timber] were four-feet high," Shafer explains, describing the stacks of cut wood that were stored in Quakish Lake before moving on to the mill to be made into pulp. The weight of the logs above was often too much for the timbers that were first to arrive. "That log on the bottom," says Shafer, "is gonna sink."

Other trees dropped to the floor of the West Branch because they had hollow cavities caused by disease and decay. "We don't call it rot," says Shafer. "We call it patina—people love the patina." And some simply became tangled in the great jams created by moving thousands of timbers at a time and were essentially wrestled below the surface. Millions of cords of wood rest in watery repose not far below the surface of the West Branch.

Now, crews working for Shafer and Sanders extract tons of sodden pine and spruce, hemlock and fir, using cranes from the lake surface to pull them from the depths, like the Claw Machine at the arcade. Then Maine Heritage Timber turns Maine's old-growth forest, century-old by-product of the state's lumbering and paper industries, into flooring, furniture, custom installations for high-end businesses, and a clever new wall application that Shafer expects to revolutionize home decor.

Before Tom Shafer could begin salvaging Maine's heritage, though, he had to reclaim his own. Sort of. When the New Jersey native ventured north from his Manhattan home in 2010, it was supposed to be temporary. He left his job on Wall Street, where he'd been working on the floor of the Stock Exchange manufacturing markets for close to twenty years, riding the ups and downs of bulls and bears. He was quite good at his job and climbed the corporate ranks, getting his seed in 1993 and becoming a partner in 1995. He had a house in Connecticut, an apartment in Manhattan, a wife and family.

It sniffs of the All-American Dream, just the kind of life he imagined for himself as a kid growing up in New Jersey. His father had worked on Wall Street, and Tom thought it was the way for him as well. "At his wake, I asked his partner for a job, and started working summers when I was sixteen." The young Shafer finished high school and went on to Denison University in Ohio, where he pitched for the Division III baseball team and studied history.

But there was another side to Tom Shafer—and to his father before him. They both loved the woods. Tom's mother was a Clark, whose family owns an island in the middle of Lower Togue Pond, a four-hundred-acre basin in the dense forest fastness of Maine's North Woods. This is the land of Katahdin, a place where woodland creatures outnumber people by exponential amounts. Access to the island is achieved by traveling through "forever wild" Baxter State Park, one of the largest wilderness areas in the east.

As a kid, Shafer spent a couple weeks a year on the island, staying in primitive family cabins with no phones, no electricity, no running water. The weathered gray camps were beautiful and simple and about as far from the corridors of power in New York as one could possibly get.

"The only vacation [my father] ever took was two weeks up here," says Shafer. "He loved that place." Young Tom loved it, too.

This North Woods idyll was where everything changed for him. Shafer's marriage dissolved in 2003 in the difficult years after 9/11. "9/11 was a very bad time," he says. He made it another five years in Manhattan. By this time he was on the board of his company when a new chairman arrived and wanted to reduce the size of the organization. Shafer saw the proverbial writing.

"I left the company thinking I'd find another job pretty easily— in 2008," he says. "I thought I'd be making a million bucks a year."

But the economy thought otherwise.

After leaving the company, Shafer played a lot of golf, hung out with his two boys, and began thinking about what his next steps should be. His uncle called and asked him to oversee construction of a new camp on their tiny island. Shafer didn't think so. "I had to find a new job," he explains. But his uncle didn't want to hear that and kept after him, eventually offering him $5,000 a month. Shafer finally relented. "At that point," he says, "I needed money." He figured he'd go home to the island, spend a few months on the project, and return to Manhattan.

It didn't work out that way.

On the site, he met Steve Sanders, who was part of the construction crew. While Tom Shafer often refers to himself as an "asshole from New York," Sanders is every bit the Maine mill town boy. His father used to cut wood to sell to Great Northern Paper Company (GNP), hauling it from the forest by horse. Sanders worked for Great Northern, and he spent time in construction in Portland, before returning to Millinocket in 2009. He's prone to shirts with no sleeves and keeps a bottle next to his desk as a spittoon.

While working on Clark Island, the pair got to talking. Sanders had been hired by Great Northern in 2002 to raise logs from the bottom of Quakish Lake. The massive international papermaking conglomerate had literally put Millinocket on the map, building the town street by street at the turn of the previous century. When it opened in 1900, Great Northern's Millinocket facility was the largest paper mill in the world, and its big biomass boiler was the beating heart of the community. Locals like to say that kids in Millinocket graduated from high school one day and started at the mill the next; it was the way of life in this corner of Maine for generations. By 1977, Great Northern had more than forty-two hundred millworkers on the books and was the state's largest private employer behind shipbuilder Bath Iron Works. The mill boomed, riding high on miles of newsprint a day, and so did the community, earning the nickname "Magic City."

Great Northern kept its timber pooled in Quakish Lake, about a mile and a half from its mill, where it would stay moist for processing. As it sat, the bottom timbers inevitably sank due to pressure from above, and the company was aware that probably thousands of cords sat down there. "They'd done some bathymetric work," says Sanders, surveying the silty floor. GNP figured at best the wood could be hauled up and dried out, and be worked into its pulper. At worst, they could write it off and claim it as an expense. Sanders was part of a team hired to dredge it up.

But Great Northern could never figure out how to clean the wood, which had been sitting submerged in mud for centuries. When it was pulled up, it was caked in antique filth. Or perhaps they never cared enough to pursue it, and eventually abandoned the idea.

Sanders didn't. He was captivated by the notion that there was a forgotten forest at the bottom of the West Branch, money sitting on the river floor. He went off to work construction in Portland but the notion never went away. Ever the history buff, Shafer was taken with the idea, too. "It's everybody's heritage," he says.

The unlikely pair—the one a market maker from Manhattan, the other a builder and jack-of-all-trades from Millinocket—figured there had to be a way to monetize the stuff. They decided to go in together and reclaim the logs.

"The original plan was to sell it back to the mill and keep the long stuff," Shafer explains. Most of the wood would become pulp, but lengthier pieces could be turned into saleable products. "We'd get some pre–Civil War wood and be gentlemen sawyers and do some furniture." They formed a corporation, and brought aboard an investor—Tom's uncle.

Great Northern had other plans. The Millinocket mill ceased operations over the course of the 2000s, starting and stopping, and sputtering out like a vehicle running out of fuel. The East Millinocket mill pressed on for a few more years, printing paper for the novel *Fifty Shades of Gray* (it was published on one shade of Great Northern's Baxter Bright paper) before it too shuttered in 2011. The blows were staggering to Millinocket, and like so many individuals and businesses in town, Maine Heritage Timber suffered.

Shafer and Sanders had to rethink their options. Nobody wanted pulp logs, and most of the timbers were too short for their crane operators to do much with.

"What do you do with a four-foot log?" was the question that immediately faced the pair. "Great Northern switched from tree length to four foot logs in 1916," says Sanders. "And most of what we find is from that boom period."

The logs weren't long enough for big furniture, beams, siding, or much else, so Shafer and Sanders started with flooring. Most of what they found on the bottom was spruce and fir—the staples of the pulp and paper industry. But they also found a fair bit of pine—Great Northern's biomass boilers didn't discriminate, melting all kinds of softwood down to become pulp, turning all these trees into *Reader's Digest* and phonebooks and the *New York Times*. For a time, the company produced more than 15 percent of all newsprint in the nation. Like the rest, the timbers of *Pinus strobus* were perfectly preserved, due to the cold temperatures, lack of air, and the fact that many of the pests and fungi that eat wood can't swim. "There isn't enough oxygen down there to begin decomposition," says Sanders.

The wood was in such great shape it was as if it had been stored there by the river drivers of yore to be pulled up later, like a time capsule. There were literal hills of it, small mountains spread across the river bottom. Once the wood was cleaned of the mud and silt that clung to it, and dried in a kiln, Shafer and Sanders found it could be worked like any other freshly felled tree.

"Softwood is easier and quicker than green wood," says Sanders. "It dries very quickly."

And decades resting on the bottom of the West Branch gave the lumber an added benefit. "When we saw it, it's this rich pink color. When we kiln dry it turns this merlot color," says Sanders. "Once we get to sawing them, it's just absolutely beautiful," agrees Shafer.

The pair used the antique pine to create an ingenious flooring. The top quarter-inch is a veneer of reclaimed wood; underneath is a half-inch layer of 11-ply Baltic birch engineered for strength. The floors can withstand the same beating as their all-wood cousins, though Shafer doesn't recommend it for very-high-traffic areas like a hall or a kitchen. It's better suited to dining rooms or living areas. Using only a small fraction of pine on top makes the timbers they pull up last longer, and the combination makes for a more durable floor than softwood alone. The old English mast makers would have nodded in astonishment at this combination of Baltic and New England timber, laminated together to create fine flooring.

But Maine Heritage Timber found their tongue and groove boards had a hard time finding space on the floors of America. "The flooring market is 91 percent oak," says Shafer, "and if you look at solid vs engineered it's like 93 percent to 7 percent. . . . When you're trying to sell a pine engineered floor, you're going after 2 percent of the market, and it's hard."

And it's simply costly—margins are as fine as the needle of a pine. "First of all, it costs $3.85 to manufacture it into engineered flooring, probably another $3 worth of costs when you take out everything else, and we're selling it for $10."

The Penobscot Collection of pine flooring is still part of Shafer and Sanders's product line, but it's now being eclipsed by other ventures, just as the pine forests of old gave way to spruce and hemlock. They'll continue to produce it, but Shafer says he has no serious plans for it. "We don't push flooring as much as we used to. People come to us if they want pine flooring. We don't have to sell it."

With engineered pine a hard sell, the company found itself having to pivot once again. "You get your master's in marketing on the fly," Shafer says.

He and Sanders were lucky to have an investor who believed in them, who stood by them when their fortunes fell like a cut timber. Shafer didn't want his uncle involved originally, but "he pushed and pushed and pushed and thank God he did, because if we had a syndicate involved, which was the original plan, we would have been closed within six months because our business plan was completely changed."

Part of the great appeal of Maine Heritage Timber, of course, is the story behind it. Not just Shafer's own tale of leaving Wall Street, or Sander's story of finding a forest underneath a back-country river, but the chronicle of the Maine woods. The epic odyssey of the timber industry of New England. The romance of the river drivers and the uniqueness of owning a piece of the North Woods that's been sitting on the bottom of the mighty Penobscot for decades. If potential customers don't buy into the intrigue of Maine Heritage Timber then they simply see prices that are slightly higher and walk away. "A lot of people don't even understand why the wood is in the river," Shafer says. "It happens all the time."

"I talked to a woman on the phone today about how we salvage submerged wood," Sanders says, "and she asked me what all those houses were doing out on the water." He shakes his head. The administrative assistant glances over from her desk with a look that shows she can't believe anyone could be so dim but at the same time understands the reaction completely because she's heard it so many times.

But many people do buy into the intrigue, and Maine Heritage Timber has found a hardy customer base who appreciate what they're selling. They've done a lot of custom installations in restaurants—from River Driver's on Millinocket Lake to Blaze in Bangor to Moxie Kitchen and Cocktails in Florida. LL Bean ordered up wood for commemorative canoe paddles to celebrate its centennial. Shafer and Sanders have found a wealth of repeat buyers who return simply because of the story and vintage and patina of the wood.

For Tom Shafer, history is value added, an integral part of his product base. He points out a cookie—a thin cutting of the trunk that's the size of a wall clock—hanging on the wall of the company's main office. "That piece of maple started growing in 1563," he says. "People just don't realize the amount of building up and down the Eastern Seaboard done with wood that came from Maine."

Not only is the company trading on the past, it draws a direct line between the men and women of today's Millinocket and the thousands of timber cutters who worked the North Woods before them. "Everybody here has worked in the woods. The guys all have a real appreciation for how hard it is to work for this," Shafers says, pointing at a reclaimed log.

And, of course, they're doing it in a green, sustainable manner. Shafer is proud of this. Anyone who strolls up to Maine Heritage Timber's facilities on the Golden Road, unaware where the wood came from, would think they are simply another company in the lumber business. Trucks come and go all the time loaded with logs; saws run all day cutting wood into salable goods. Yet they haven't felled a single tree. Shafer estimates that they save about a thousand acres from being cut every year.

Shafer is also keen to provide good jobs for seventeen people who would undoubtedly have serious difficulty finding other employment in the failing economy of a dying mill town. The demise of Great Northern in Millinocket has been a disaster for the community. Vacant homes and storefronts are everywhere, there are hardly enough kids to fill classrooms, drugs and theft are far more commonplace than they once were. Many in town hold out hope that the woods economy will be revived—the argument was bandied about again with the arrival of a new national monument to woodlands once owned by timber companies like Irving and Bowater—but it's been proven empirically again and again that pulp trees can grow faster in southern and Asian climes.

And the everyday people of Millinocket still look askance at Maine Heritage Timber, Shafer says. Much like the people from away who feel terrible about all those houses falling into the river, they can't wrap their head around what Shafer and Sanders are doing. Many see it as the quixotic quest of an asshole from New York. "They still think I'm crazy," Shafer explains. "'Oh, you're the crazy bastard who's doing that project.' But when Millinocket is the home of Timberchic, they'll say, 'That crazy son of a bitch knew something.'"

Shafer and Sanders have high hopes for the Timberchic line they introduced in March 2016. "What do you do with a four-foot-long log?" Shafer asks rhetorically. "We found out what to do with it. It's called Timberchic."

Much like their earlier ventures in pine flooring and wainscoting, the new product is a decorative veneer, in this case a clever peel-and-stick wood grain application—like a very thin wood tile—to create accent walls. Any homeowner handy with a chalk line and a level can give a room a rustic look in an afternoon with little skill needed. Timbers that were once shepherded down the West Branch by river drivers are cut into millimeter-thick strips, backed with tape, and sold in long narrow boxes to reclaim boring bedrooms and kitchen walls.

The launch has been slow but steady. "It's really hard to do it without a bring-to-market program," says Shafer, "without being able to spend $25,000 a month on PR, being on the *Today Show*, but we just can't afford it."

Timberchic seems to be winning fans all by itself. Sales are doubling by the month, and the reviews have been great. "It is so unbelievable," says Shafer. "We don't get any returns. We have, like 50 percent repeat customers. People love it." The company produces about forty boxes of the self-adhering boards a day, by hand. "We'll sell 500 boxes in a month, easily, easily, within six months."

Maine Heritage Timber thinks Timberchic will soon be paying almost all the bills. "Right now it's about 40-60 revenue-wise," says Shafer. "It's going to be 90-10 soon. In two years, I guarantee it."

At the moment, Shafer and Sanders and their crew are working almost entirely on preparing Timberchic's mixed-wood line of products, and the New Jersey pitcher remains excited. "We'll be all right," he says. "As long as I have the passion we'll be fine."

The North Woods couldn't be much farther removed from Manhattan, but Tom Shafer is glad to be back, close to his family heritage on Clark Island. "This is so much more rewarding than anything I ever did in New York," he says. "It's not about the bottom line. Everything in New York was about the bottom line. This is about reviving a history nobody really knows about, providing jobs for seventeen people in a shithole of a town. . . . Instilling a little entrepreneurship in this area, is really really important."

CHAPTER TWELVE

Treeconomics

From the pine tree, learn of the pine tree.

—BASHO

GROWING UP OBSESSED WITH BASKETBALL IN THE TINY WOODS-and-lakes town of Casco, Maine, Kevin Hancock never really considered going into the family business—one of the oldest family-owned companies in the nation. Along with his brother, Matt, the young Kevin was all about hoops, and the two boys went about making the Hancock name famous for other reasons, regularly filling newspaper sports columns with their exploits on the courts for Lakes Region High School. They won places in the Lakers' Hall of Fame, and led the Lakers to the Class B state championships, picking up Class B Player of the Year Awards along the way. (Cousin Mike Shane, too, was a local basketball great.) After high school, Kevin went fifty miles down the road to Bowdoin College, where he was captain of the NCAA Division III team and set scoring records. Younger brother Matt put up more points than any other college basketball player in state history during his career at Colby in the late eighties, and was invited to camps for both the Celtics and the Golden State Warriors.

The Hancock family's legacy never really factored into Kevin's plans. As a college student, he studied history and considered a career in teaching or coaching or both. It wasn't that he didn't want to do what his father and grandfather did—what five generations of Hancocks did—he simply had his own plans. "I didn't say, 'I'd never do that,' he explains, "[it] never actually crossed my mind." And to his credit, the Hancock boys' father, David, president of the company, never put any pressure on them to follow his path. He was a basketball great himself.

As anyone from southern Maine knows, the Hancock family business is trees—specifically eastern white pines. Hancock Lumber is the world's largest producer of white pine boards. ("It would either be us or Irving. We're both always right there [annually]," says Hancock.) Thin boards, wide boards, clapboards, barn boards, primed finish boards—they manufacture it all. The company is an institution in Cumberland County, one of the region's biggest employers, with 475 employees working in ten stores, three sawmills, and twelve thousand rare acres of timberlands in the state's most populous corner. And it has been for a long time—the business was started before the Civil War just a few tree lengths from the lakeside spot in downtown Casco where Hancock Lumber's administrative offices now sit.

Kevin Hancock's father, David, was president of the company from 1976 to 1998, his grandfather was at the helm before him, and his grandfather's grandfather further back—the line straight from father to son for six generations. If Kevin and his brother, Matt, decided to continue coaching and playing basketball, instead of reporting for duty with filial piety, Hancock might well have been without a Hancock at the helm for the first time since Sumner O. Hancock took control of the lumber business his father-in-law began in 1848.

"There were a lot of people who looked at me and my brother and thought for sure that's what we were going to do when we grew up," says Hancock. If the company were called Decker Lumber, a much more likely candidate than Hancock Lumber when the business was founded during the Polk administration, no one outside the immediate family would likely have given much mind to whether Kevin and Matt wanted in. But it wasn't, and it's not clear why.

The evergreen roots of Hancock Lumber were planted when Nathan and Spencer Decker agreed to pay Ambrose Wright $850 for a lumber mill he had set up in the village of Casco, hard by the shore of aptly named Pleasant Lake. The brothers forked over $100 initially, and then paid out the remainder in installments, once they had their blades spinning. This was at the end of the heyday of the white pine era in the Pine Tree State. Thoreau had written his treatise on the Maine Woods, and the supply of the conifer was slowly petering out in the forests north of Bangor. Most of the big trees were gone, leaving just shag bark and chips in their wake, but the Decker brothers evidently saw some promise in the woodlands of the Sebago Lake area, and they decided they'd make a go of a mill.

Forty miles to the northwest of Falmouth, the area around Casco has always had a lumbering tradition. The king's surveyors pored through the woods around the community identifying the king's pines, and locals have made their living with axes and saws since the eighteenth century. When the town grew large enough to have its own high school, the sports teams were called the Casco Loggers, with axes on their uniforms.

In 1848, a lumber company seemed a reasonable proposition. Homes were going in all over the place in the new State of Maine, and pine was the favored material for construction. Light and strong and easily worked, it was used as sheathing, flooring, moulding, all over the capes and Georgians being built. John Holden and his son, Frank, had been running a water-powered sawmill at the outlet of Pleasant Lake for a decade already and seemed to be making a fair go.

Nathan and Spencer Decker worked to build up the business—they had mouths to feed. Nathan had taken a wife, Hannah Stuart Hancock, who was the widow of Sumner O. Hancock and already had a son, Sumner O. Hancock Jr. Decker raised the boy as his own, but for some reason little Sumner never changed his surname, a common thing to do at the time.

When Sumner O. Hancock Jr. grew up, he took over the business the Deckers had started, grew it exponentially, and gave it his name. He bought timberlands, began using portable sawmills in the woods, and built the company into the largest lumber supplier in Cumberland County by the 1880s, with four thousand acres and fifteen teams of men working for him. His sons Milton and Ralph both entered the family business, and Milton would take over after Sumner.

"The simple way I think about it is that we've doubled the company," Kevin Hancock says, pausing, then adds, "twice." Today, Hancock is sitting in his office in the corporate headquarters of Hancock Lumber in Casco. At fifty, he still has a boyish face, with narrow eyes, as if he's always thinking, and a wide smile. He's imposing, well over six foot, and it's not hard to imagine him driving the lane for a layup in his younger days. On the walls are the elk heads he's taken on his travels—hunting is a new pastime—along with decrees from the Maine State Legislature honoring the company, family photos, and, of course, amber-colored pine.

After college Hancock took a job teaching history—and coaching basketball—at Bridgton Academy. In 1991, he was planning on entering the University of Maine's School of Law when he got some disturbing news. "That summer my dad was diagnosed with cancer," he says. Hancock felt the need to go home, and took a job in the company at the retail end, waiting on customers in the Yarmouth store. And he never left, moving up the ranks. Within a year, he was managing the Windham store. By 1995, he was the general manager of the company's entire retail division. When his father died the following year, he assumed his place in the family line.

"I was sure I was ready for it," he says with a laugh. "I was sure it wasn't that complicated—thinking like a thirty-year-old." He soon absorbed the basics and began to grow the company. Eight stores became ten. Hancock added a third mill. Everything was on the ups from the time he took over in 1998 for the next eight years. Housing starts were multiplying exponentially in southern Maine, New Hampshire, and the rest of New England during the late '90s, and Hancock's fortunes were very directly nailed to them. "When housing is booming our company tends to grow very quickly," he says.

The company was moving steadily in the right direction like the pine boards on conveyors in Hancock's Ryefield mill. "We grew quite a bit every year during that period," he says. "I like to joke about it now but we thought [the expanding balloon of the southern Maine housing market] was us. The only economy I'd know at that point was that next year's bigger."

The young executive soon found out that it was not Hancock Lumber driving the economy and that economies don't always have to grow. The foundation was rudely pulled from under the housing business by Wall Street and its fictional mortgages. Hancock found his entire empire wobbled. "It was a violent, violent crash in the market," he says. "Housing starts in southern Maine fell by 66 percent from 2007 to 2010." Hancock Lumber's sale of pine boards tumbled off a cliff with them, dropping by 50 percent, "without ever losing a customer," as Hancock wryly puts it. "The same people who were with us before were with us after."

All those millions of pine boards the company so efficiently produces, of course, go into the construction of homes and businesses, and when no homes and businesses are being built, they simply sit in warehouses. Lowe's and Home Depot, building supply stores in Maine, and contractors all over, stopped calling for more. Suddenly Hancock had to start looking at downsizing and economizing. "When housing retrenches, our business tends to shrink rather quickly," Hancock explains.

The downturn hit Hancock Lumber hard, and Kevin Hancock felt it on a personal level. His world was about to change yet again.

"In 2010, at the peak of the housing market collapse, I began to have trouble speaking." The young CEO found his voice was gone. "When I went to talk all the muscles in my throat would squeeze and spasm and contract, and my voice would get very weak and broken." He could barely make himself heard. For a corporate executive used to making speeches and running meetings in boardrooms it was a shock.

"I found myself wondering how I would help lead a lumber company through that economy without consistently being able to use my voice."

Doctors told Hancock he had spasmodic dysphonia, a neurological ailment that causes the larynx to spasm involuntarily, making the voice sound broken or strangled. The disorder strikes gradually, without any apparent cause or damage to the larynx. An estimated fifty thousand people suffer from spasmodic dysphonia in North America, though physicians think the numbers might be much higher.

Hancock found he couldn't make the speeches he once did, couldn't issue the orders that he once had, and, typical of the boy from Casco, he figured out a workaround. "When you can't always talk a lot, you get very good at listening," he says. It was a transformative moment for the young executive. Staff would come to him and tell him they had a problem and wait for his orders. Instead, he would ask them what they thought. "People had great answers. I came to see really quickly that they knew [what to do]."

The simple act of listening changed Hancock—and the lumber company that bears his name—forever. "I came to see a pretty powerful opportunity in losing some of my voice, which was to strengthen the voices of others," he says. He had a bit of an epiphany. "What if we could create an organization where everybody leads, where every voice was a key leading voice? Wouldn't an organization where everybody leads actually outperform and be more dynamic and valuable than a traditional organization, especially a family business, where just a few people did all the big talking, controlled all the big meetings, made all the big decisions?"

He would find out.

If one of the loggers from Ebenezer Mudgett's sawmill in Weare, New Hampshire, walked into the New Hampshire woods 150 years later, he'd probably feel pretty much at home. Felling a pine still required axes, though the two-man crosscut saw, sometimes referred to as a "misery whip," was also widely used and replaced the ax in some operations. Trees were still cut in winter by men living in lumber camps, oxen were still used to tug tree-length boles to towering piles on riverbanks, and spring freshets were still used to drive the lumber to mills. In those sawmills, steam may have replaced water as the source of power for the spinning blades, but that would have been seen as a nifty innovation, not a mind bogglement.

If that time-traveling timber cutter walked into Hancock's woodlands today and followed trees to Hancock Lumber's Rye-field Mill in Casco, Maine, however, the experience would be altogether alien. The felling of a pine in 2016 is wholly different than it was even fifty years ago. Like every other industry, the pine lumber business has been mechanized. Machines do the work at every step. Feller bunchers do the cutting now, tall, brutally efficient vehicles with massive saws in huge pincher claws attached to thirty-foot crane arms, and wide, grinding tracks that roll through the woods like tanks. Operators sit inside climate-controlled cabs, controlling the arms with joysticks while watching along on computers, like playing video games. The machines are capable of cutting, limbing, and bucking all at once. When the timber is stripped and ready, it's loaded on the back of a twenty-five-ton logging truck.

Truckers drive many of the tree-length pine logs to Hancock's Ryefield Mill for processing. "The majority of the wood is from

WHITE PINE

a fifty-mile radius," says mill manager Mike Shane, cousin to the Hancock brothers and former b-ball great himself. "We are in the heart of pine country here." And the pines do indeed define rural Route 11 in every direction, surrounding the countless lakes and ponds of Maine's lakes region, and riding the hills up to the sky. The area is home to forty-seven-square-mile Sebago Lake, hundreds of smaller ponds, dozens of summer camps, and thousands of summer homes.

Ryefield Mill doesn't look much from the road. House-sized piles of white pine sit out front, massive tangles of brown that reach up more than a story. Outdoor conveyors give a hint of the purpose of the place. On a huge steel facade, under a wooden Hancock Lumber sign (a sawblade taking the place of the "O,") is another sign that proclaims: "Manufacturing Stays in This Country." Below that is a "Now Hiring" banner, which proudly mentions that the company was recognized in 2014 as one of the best places to work in Maine. Off to one side of the entryway are the mill's offices, the only structures on this sprawling campus that don't scream or grind or pound from within.

In the mill itself, the pines are very loudly rendered unrecognizable. They go in one end through a metal detector—the teeth of the mill's blades can't take nails or spikes or anything but wood grain in the bole—and emerge from the other in the form of boards. For the size of the mill and the amount of wood it produces—"we'll do 900 to 1,000 logs a day," says Shane, and "26 to 27 million board feet a year"—relatively few people work inside. Most steps of the transformation from tree to board are automated.

The fragrant pines don't stand a chance against the technology inside. Red laser eyes are everywhere, reading, scanning, and assessing, making millions of digital decisions per second. Wood is constantly being measured and judged and moved onto the appropriate conveyor by computer arms. Big blonde beams surf along chain pathways toward machines like the Esterer sash gang saw, a monster with vicious vertical blades that cut wood like a big

140

bread slicer, making thousands of cuts per minute. They pass by edge-mounted saws to trim excess, and get shaved. In one booth, an operator looks at video screens as sensors take measurements; he'll determine how to get the most usable material from a log, cutting off imperfections, based on computer data and camera angles. At another station a sawyer uses an iPad to control the horizontal trimmer. "We look for any opportunity to upgrade the value of the board," explains Shane.

Scraps fall at each stage, conveyed out. Depending on their size, they'll become clean pine shavings for animal bedding—"sorted for size and quality as well," says the mill manager—or sold as biomass to paper mills. The bark is trucked to a New Hampshire firm that grinds it and uses it for landscaping. Low-grade seconds or thirds get sent to Asia. "What they do overseas is amazing," says Shane. "They'll cut sections of premium wood out and it will go to Pakistan or somewhere and come back as a picture frame you'll see in Walmart." The green sawdust stays right at Ryefield and is pumped into a boiler in the kiln, where the wood is dried. "Everything on that log we're using."

It's a massive operation, and still growing—contractors are installing more sorting capacity in the form of new conveyors through an additional steel structure. And it's not even as big as Hancock Lumber's Bethel mill. Technology reigns supreme. Shane points out wryly that, although a lot of the massive machinery is twenty or thirty years old, the mill faces the same issue as the average homeowner: "It's the software you have to keep upgrading."

But the mill wasn't always so busy. As the housing market slowed, its conveyors did, too. Kevin Hancock tried to think of solutions. And his listening epiphany was soon followed by another one. In 2012, he picked up a copy of the August issue of *National Geographic* and read a piece on the Pine Ridge Reservation in South Dakota. This was the land of the mighty Sioux, the great cavalry warriors who gave the U.S. government fits in the mid-nineteenth century, filling the nation's plans of manifest destiny with arrows. "The Sioux on the northern plains and the Comanche on the southern plains pretty much stopped westward expansion for twenty years," Hancock says.

As an avid reader of history, he knew a little about the tribe, having read the classic *Bury My Heart at Wounded Knee.* These were the brave warriors who fought Custer. The tribe of Crazy Horse, and Sitting Bull, and Red Cloud, who tormented the U.S. Army in a series of wars on the plains, and made headlines again in the 1970s for the AIM protests at Wounded Knee. Reading the piece in *National Geographic* Hancock found himself curious about the tribe today. What became of the noble Sioux nation?

"Without a lot of thought, I said to my wife, 'I'm going to go there.'"

He made the nineteen-hundred-mile journey from the pine woods of Maine to Pine Ridge Reservation in Oglala Lakota County and found it to be healing, a "way to reconnect with the other sides of who I was that had not really been needed or called on in my family business," he says. "I'd hit a point in my life where I wanted to define myself more broadly than just my company leadership role."

As he traveled around the historic reservation, he scribbled his thoughts in a journal that became tattered with use, filling it with characters he met and ideas he formed. He snapped photo after photo. He was struck by the poverty, depression, and darkness around him, but he also learned, absorbing Sioux ways, picking up words and phrases from their language, and making many friends. Because he didn't attempt to tell them how they should live—just listened—the stoic Sioux eventually warmed to the New England CEO. Hancock wanted to find a way to help if he could, without imposing. He was captivated by the people and their landscape. "One trip turned into two and then ten," he says.

Hancock turned his journals into a book: *Not for Sale: Finding Center in the Land of Crazy Horse.* A 512-page meditation, it's a travelogue, memoir, and metaphysical treatise on business all in one. In the foreword, Maine Senator Angus King, a friend of Hancock's, writes: "If you had told me a couple of years ago that my friend, Kevin Hancock, would set off on a quest for enlightenment, sparked by a long-distance astrological reading which would lead him to a sweat lodge in a remote Indian reservation well, let's just say that skeptical doesn't come close to covering it."

The young executive found great inspiration in what he saw around him. "I came to see, in the old ways of the Sioux, what I thought was a path forward for me, them, Hancock Lumber, and possibly—as big as this sounds—for humanity." What impressed Hancock most was the power and the importance of the individual. He points out how confused the natives were when the U.S. government showed up and asked to speak to the tribe's leader. "Nobody knew what that meant," Hancock says. "Surely no one spoke for everyone."

Because each individual in the tribe was strong and had a voice, the tribe was strong. "It's right out of Rudyard Kipling's *The Jungle Book*," he explains. "The strength of the pack is the wolf."

Surely a company could benefit from this idea? "What the book is really about is leadership in the Aquarian Age being about restraint—having the power to do all the talking, run every meeting, make all the decisions—but not using it."

Upon his return from Pine Ridge, Hancock began to implement some of his ideas, which sound more like those emanating from the boardrooms of Apple and Microsoft and Google than they do from a Maine lumber baron, a man whose livelihood is, while technologically advanced, not too far from that of the New England mill owners who defied the crown in the eighteenth century. Hancock took the old corporate triangle of shareholders, employees, and customers and inverted it so that employees come first, then customers, and shareholders last.

"That old saying, 'the customer comes first,' I don't think that's right. I think the customer comes a really close second. The people who are going to take care of that customer come first." The staff who make, handle, and represent the product, he says, are paramount. "If you take care of them, they will take great care of the resource and the customer."

Empowering employees was the key. No longer would the company function like corporations of old, with a trickle-down mentality, where ideas and information and direction all came from the top, and most of the money stayed there. Everyone who worked for Hancock Lumber would have a voice and their efforts would be rewarded. Incentive-based programs were put in place. The work week shrunk—and yet people earn the same. "If people can work a little bit less and earn a little bit more," says Hancock, "that's directionally the right path."

Hancock's new direction has been recognized at the state level. The company has been named among the best places to work in Maine, and sales are up to about $150 million a year. But there are some things about manufacturing lumber that simply can't be changed.

"It's the craziest business," Kevin Hancock says. "If you weren't already in it, you'd probably never go into it." No matter how a CEO changes the corporate culture, expands his operations, implements best practices, and perfects sales, he can't make his product grow faster. Especially if that product is the eastern white pine. "Our company has been in business since 1848," he explains, "and we've had two crops." It takes eighty years for a tiny pine seedling to grow into a mature tree ready to be felled and ripped into boards. Hancock likes to joke with a friend who runs a farm stand in Casco, and sells corn and beans and pumpkins. "I'll say, 'You plant these in the spring and you harvest them in the fall? What a great idea.'"

There simply isn't any way to introduce efficiencies into the growth cycle. "The only thing you have to do to grow more pine trees is—nothing," Hancock says. "You just have to do it for a long time."

Hancock Lumber does a little more than not at all. The company works hard to give the pines on their lands the best chance possible to mature into an exceptional evergreen. The company's woodcutters approach things quite differently than the harvesters of the king's pine era. They'll cut some of the trees, leave most of the trees, and purposefully leave some good seed trees. They open the canopy, allowing in more sunlight, and churn up the forest floor, making the soil very fertile and ready to grow.

The best individual pines will go untouched, left behind to drop their huge cones. "We don't do any replanting or any genetic engineering. There is some, I guess I would call, mechanical engineering," the CEO says. "Where we're taking out more of the less desirable tree and leaving more of the higher value trees—and those built-in genetics." The idea is that these impressive specimens will sire a new generation of fine pines. It's the antithesis of the broad arrow days. Hancock explains that he pays people to care for seedlings "in the hope that eighty years from now that might be a harvestable crop."

Not only does his crop take ages to grow, but the pines of today have some serious competition. Boards for the housing market can be made from a wide variety of trees, from the southern pine to the ponderosa pine of the American west to European spruce, and the radiata pine of South America and New Zealand. The radiata, in particular, is a valiant opponent, growing on vast plantations—farms, really—where they're shepherded along and then cut in mass quantities—and compared to their northerly cousins, they mature fast.

"One of the challenges for white pines—I think the radiata pine can grow to harvest in 20–25 years," Hancock says. "So we're competing with other resources in warm climates that have a faster cycle." But speed isn't everything. Those other trees may be quicker to market, but the pine is simply better. "The cool thing is that all of those different species have certain attributes that determine their value and while the overall market can have a lot of movement, the white pine is always at the top, value wise."

And one of the regions it grows best happens to surround his home. Luckily for Kevin Hancock, and the company that bears his name, white pine are just as valuable in 2016 as they were when George Weymouth first stood in wonder of them in 1605. "White pine only grows, in critical mass for global manufacturing quantities, in a very few places on Earth, and one of the best happens to be . . ." He points outside the office. And smiles.

CHAPTER THIRTEEN

If a Tree Falls

Acts of creation are ordinarily reserved for gods and poets, but humbler folk may circumvent this restriction if they know how. To plant a pine, for example, one need be neither god nor poet; one need only own a good shovel.

—ALDO LEOPOLD[1]

WHEN GENERAL CHRISTOPHER COLUMBUS ANDREWS ISSUED his warning in August 1894, nobody listened. As a prominent Minnesota resident, he'd kept a keen eye on the way the lumber companies were conducting their business, and he didn't approve. Growing up in New Hampshire he remembered winter days walking through evergreen forests, "felling smaller trees and clearing the land carefully sparing young white pines," as he put it in his autobiography. By contrast, the lumbermen he saw around him in the vast pine woods of Minnesota spared nothing. Despite the fact that they'd seen the pines of Maine fall, followed by the pineries of New York, Pennsylvania, and Wisconsin, timber barons didn't slow their cutting efforts. By 1890, the state was shipping billions of board feet of white pine, cutting with fury and abandon. Westward expansion was under way—the population of the United States more than doubled between the end of the Civil War and the turn of the twentieth century—and all those settlers needed building materials. Trees fell and fell. The thinking was, the forests were infinite, and where they were clear cut, farmers could simply move in and make productive pastures.

But that wasn't necessarily what was bothering General Andrews. He didn't like that Minnesota lumber companies were dropping trees and then simply leaving the undesirable boughs and branches where they fell, creating a thick, ready-to-burn blanket that spread for tens of thousands of acres. Dry and brittle, piled up deep, it was the perfect kindling for a forest conflagration. A passing train, a well-aimed lightning strike, and the devastation would be vast. The timber cutters took all the trees, and nothing was replanted to add stability and moisture to the landscape.

That hot August at a meeting of foresters in Brooklyn, the general pointed this out.

And his opinion mattered. He was a respected and accomplished individual, serving valiantly in the Civil War, where he entered as a private in 1861 and mustered out in 1866 as a major general. He'd been a Minnesota state senator, started a newspaper, passed the bar, authored several books, and worked as a minister to Sweden, Norway, and Brazil before returning to Minnesota. He was thought of highly, but that August, his voice was drowned out by the sound of saw blades. The white pine ruled Minnesota's economy, employing more than thirty thousand lumbermen by 1901. And nobody wanted to slow down the machine.

Andrews had attended a forestry conference in Sweden, where he learned from the progressive foresters of Scandinavia, who were well ahead of their American counterparts. As far back as 1872, the general had written a sixty-six-page report about Swedish practices, and he thought Minnesota could—and should—learn from them. In August 1894, he gave a speech to the American Forestry Congress in Brooklyn, New York, entitled: Prevention of Forest Fires.

Nobody listened.

And a little over a week later came the flames.

No one was sure how the fire got started, but the woods of central Minnesota were parched that summer. For three years, the St. Paul Weather Bureau had reported drier than normal conditions, and that August was no different. Rains were few, amounting to just a couple of inches for the hottest part of the year. Twice that much was the average—per month. Some months could be closer to five inches. By September 1894, it was hot, dusty, and fires burned periodically, some started by lumber companies, some by sparks from passing rail cars, some by careless outdoorspeople.

On September 1, 1894, temperatures were in the 90s, and an inversion pressed the heat down on the small community of Hinckley in the aptly named Pine County. A lumber town of about fifteen hundred, Hinckley was located in the evergreen woods between St. Paul and Duluth. Founded as the Village of Central Station in 1885, it was transformed with the advent of rail in 1869. The arrival of the Lake Superior and Mississippi Railroad had turned it into a happening place, and it sprouted like a sapling, thanks to the endless pine woods that stretched in every direction from its small downtown. Hinckley became something of a hub for the sleepy hamlets in the region. Two railroads bisected the community, and there were hotels, a druggist, several stores, doctor's offices, and a school in town, in addition to the sawmill that employed more than two hundred. Brennan Lumber Company sprawled across almost forty acres in Hinckley, with millions of feet of pine boards stacked outside its mill, hard by the railroad. The screaming blades inside produced more than two hundred thousand board feet in the average day.

But September 1 was no average day, at least weather wise. The air was searing, thanks to the inversion parked overhead. These atmospheric events are so called because they are a bit of a scientific anomaly, the opposite of what usually happens. Normally, of course, warm air rises. In the case of an inversion, a layer of cold air sits above the heated air, pressing it to the ground.

They are famous for creating high temperatures—and even more famous for their role in wildfires.

Many historians think that it was the combination of baking heat, withered pine slash, and zero humidity that caused a pair of blazes to spontaneously erupt that morning in the cut-over pine wastelands beyond the villages of Mission Creek and Brook Park. By midday, the winds picked up and began to tear across the region. Residents of Duluth, seventy miles away, recalled the air being thick and gray and having to turn on lights in the early afternoon. The two fires somehow managed to meet, merging into a single raging blaze. It grew and grew, helped along by winds and the inversion, which kept superheated gases from rising. The conflagration drew oxygen from the air, feeding itself, and it blasted through pine slash, jumping into the trees, expanding and magnifying into a massive firestorm. Tornadoes of flame shot into the sky, soaring as high as 4.5 miles, blazing vortexes spun off it, and tongues of fire reached out and to the sides. And a towering inferno two hundred feet tall began to fly toward Hinckley.

At first, people in town could hear the roar coming from the south. Then, it seemed to simply be everywhere. Residents loaded their most beloved possessions into carts and began running north. They boarded trains, but even these iron horses had a hard time moving faster than the fire. Others sought shelter in wells, streams, ponds, and the Grindstone River. They dove into hollows, and hunkered down in the local gravel pit, covering themselves with wet blankets. One brave telegraph man, Thomas Dunn, vowed to stay at his post to keep people informed about the blaze. He died in place, transmitting the final words: "I think I've stayed too long." Even the men of Hinckley's small volunteer fire company were forced to flee.

The *New York Times* reported of the Great Fire of Hinckley, as it came to be known: "Not only was every green and living thing licked up by the flames, but the soil itself was blackened and consumed, and the earth torn up." Temperatures reached as high as two thousand degrees, melting rails, and forcing relief trains to stop in their tracks. The Brennan Lumber Company went up like a match, massive piles of lumber all but vaporized where they stood.

The blaze lasted all of four hours. But in that time, it managed to destroy Hinckley, Mission Creek, Brook Park, and three other towns, and scorched more than four hundred square miles. At least 418 people were taken by the flames, and that only accounted for residents in the larger communities. Add in people who lived in the backcountry, natives, and lumbermen working in the woods, and the death toll was probably more than five hundred. Among them was likely Thomas P. "Boston" Corbett, the born-again Union soldier who killed Lincoln's killer, John Wilkes Booth.

In the aftermath of the fire, many people were amazed at the prescience of General Andrews, and his ideas of scientific forestry were no longer seen as far-fetched. He was given the job of fire warden, the first in Minnesota, and he was also named the state's forest commissioner, again a new post. After Hinckley, commissioner Andrews argued heartily for reforestation efforts to begin, for trees to be left behind when the pines were cut, and for a new national park to protect acreage.

General Andrews was not always popular among the locals, but there were men in high places who were paying close attention to his work. Very high places. The woods had some seriously powerful friends. Every year as fire warden he published a summary of the year's events, full of problems and praise. The Fifth Annual Report of the Chief Fire Warden of Minnesota made its way onto the desk of the new U.S. Forestry commissioner, Gifford Pinchot. A confidant of President Theodore Roosevelt and power player in elite circles, Pinchot called the general's forestry law "one of the best and most progressive in force in any of the states."

Gifford Pinchot was about as able an ally as General Andrews could have found in his call for better forestry practices. Born to wealth in Simsbury, Connecticut, the rangy Pinchot was encouraged to study forestry by his father despite the fact that forestry as a profession didn't yet exist. Pinchot's father, James, was an early conservationist. His father, Cyrille, had made mountains of money on land speculation and lumbering, and to a certain extent James considered it blood money—he harbored guilt about how his family concerns had treated the landscape.

In penance, he sent young Gifford, who always loved the woods, first to Yale and then on to study at the French National School of Forestry in Nancy. Europe no longer had the woodland resources that North America had, but it was far advanced in stewardship and science-based forest management. "I had no more conception of what it meant to be a forester than the man in the moon," Pinchot would say later. "But at least a forester worked in the woods and with the woods—and I loved the woods and everything about them."

Off went Gifford to Nancy, where he pursued graduate work. Upon his return to the United States, Pinchot began to build a career in conservation. He and his father gave an endowment to the nascent Yale School of Forestry in 1900, and the family's turreted estate in Milford, Pennsylvania, became a nursery to grow trees.

At the time, the American forestry movement was but a seedling. The landscape of North America was dramatically changed from the days when George Weymouth went ashore amid two-hundred-foot pines and cut down spars for his ship. The old growth pineries had largely been destroyed, turned into boards and staves, masts and mouldings. Thanks to voices like that of General Andrews, James Pinchot, and Henry David Thoreau before them, awareness had been quietly growing that the landscape couldn't be sustained if treated the way it had been and that removing every last stick of marketable timber and reducing forests to slash and refuse was not only illogical, commercially, but was greedy and wasteful, ugly, and ultimately dangerous.

The nation was slowly waking up to the fact that the woods needed looking after. They were not, as many had previously thought, inexhaustible, trundling off to the Pacific in an endless supply. They were sensitive ecosystems, and if they were cut and left as piles of slash, they'd be nothing more than a wasteland of stumps.

In 1881 the Division of Forestry was opened in the Department of Agriculture. Five years later, the National Forest Commission was established as an offshoot of the National Academy of Sciences. Cornell added a State College of Forestry to its baccalaureate options. Pinchot himself began organizing meetings of a new trade group, the Society of American Foresters, in 1900.

By 1910, the original stands of *Pinus strobus* had fallen in Maine, Pennsylvania, New York, Minnesota, and the Lower Peninsula of Michigan. Other species, too, had been cleared, and massive stretches of the original American canopy had been opened up. Farms and pasturelands replaced woodlands across New England and out to the Midwest.

This was all a little late for the old growth pine, but it was something.

And a nascent conservation movement was growing, too. John Muir was arguing against the marketing of nature. Gifford Pinchot, and his friend, the young President Theodore Roosevelt, both believed in a new idea, sustainability, which allowed for harvesting, and even commercializing wood, but in a responsible way that left behind a healthy forest to regrow.

Unlike John Muir, Pinchot believed that the woods should be cut, but he did agree with the California conservationist that huge swaths should be held by the government so they could be managed properly. He was against preservation for the sake of preservation, but he also knew that what had been done before was not workable or efficient. Or good stewardship. Pinchot's idea was that the U.S. government would create national forests and allow private timber cutters to harvest wood within them—but under specific guidelines.

These included reforestation.

The Forest Service grew and prospered under the guidance of Pinchot and Roosevelt, and offices opened across the nation. At a desk in the Region 9 headquarters in Milwaukee, Wisconsin, sat Margaret March-Mount. March-Mount worked in public relations for the nascent organization, officially listed as an "assistant information specialist," according to the *Milwaukee Journal*. This took her into classrooms and women's clubs, promoting the planting of trees and fire safety.

Out of these informal talks came an idea—March-Mount launched a new reforestation effort called "Penny Pines." Part of a "Children's Conservation Crusade," it was a simple fund-raising mechanism—for every $4 received, the U.S. Forest Service would plant one thousand seedlings. The notion captivated the nation. Schools, garden clubs, private clubs, scout troops, all began to collect pennies, and by 1940, the USFS planted more than six million trees on six thousand acres of national forestland. Trees were planted in forty states and the District of Columbia with the help of a new conservation organization, founded by yet another President Roosevelt.

Six years earlier, in 1933, President Franklin Delano Roosevelt launched the Civilian Conservation Corps as one of the flagbearers of the New Deal. A massive public works undertaking, the CCC had as its mission environmental preservation, and tree planting was among its largest initiatives. Some called the new agency Roosevelt's "Tree Army." Set up in quasi-military fashion, under the control of the Army, the CCC grew exponentially. Within two years, more than half a million corpsmen worked in rural and remote areas across the country, living in barracks, addressing officers as "sir," and putting "planting bars" or "dibbles" to earth to plant trees. Each member was tasked with planting a thousand trees—per day. In a five-day work week, a crew of 150 could virtually grow a forest.

By the time the United States entered World War II, sending many members of the CCC off to fight—they were already disciplined young men used to taking orders and bunking in barracks—the organization had planted more than three billion trees nationwide. A great many of them were pine. Nowhere did the CCC do more work than in Michigan. Roosevelt's wilderness warriors planted 484 million trees in the Water Wonderland alone, spreading out across both peninsulas, building more than 125 camps, and replanting lands cut over by a rapacious white pine logging industry. They fought erosion, restored thousands of acres, and constructed parks and recreation areas. In its decade of life, the CCC was responsible for more than half of the reforestation done in the United States, by far more than any other organization, public or private.

In the thirties, Roosevelt's Tree Army would be called on to fight a deadly battle with the potential to be every bit as devastating as Hinckley's fire, against a new yellow invader.

Chapter Fourteen

Snags

Few are altogether deaf to the preaching of pine trees. Their sermons on the mountains go to our hearts; and if people in general could be got into the woods, even for once, to hear the trees speak for themselves, all difficulties in the way of forest preservation would vanish.

—John Muir[1]

In 1909, a young forester in Geneva, New York, leaned over to inspect a shipment of white pine seedlings from Germany, when he noticed something curious: two of the tiny evergreens had a golden growth—a swelling, it seemed—on their branches. A recent graduate of Cornell—a member of its first class of forestry students—Clifford Pettis knew this wasn't normal. Like so many other foresters, he had always admired the eastern white pine, and he'd studied the tree closely, and he could tell that these sensitive little plants, imported from a nursery in Germany, carried something that they shouldn't. Pettis immediately quarantined the affected trees and sent a telegram to the U.S. Department of Agriculture in Washington.

At the turn of the twentieth century, the U.S. government had looked to Europe, with a certain degree of irony, to buy perfect *Pinus strobus* seedlings to help replant the vast forests of America. As the forestry movement was beginning to take root in America—and the nation began to heed the warnings of Andrews and Pinchot—the white pine seedling stock of America was exhausted. The tiny trees were being planted at a rate faster than nurseries growing for seed could keep up. Thus foresters sent for seedlings from nurseries in France and Germany and Holland.

The European trees were, in fact, descended from American *Pinus strobus*. In 1705, white pine seeds had been sent from America to Longleat, the sprawling manse at Bath, England, of Thomas Tynne, the 1st Viscount of Weymouth. Tynne thought he could grow eastern white pines on his massive estate and sell them to the Royal Navy. (Some say the term *Weymouth pine* comes from Tynne rather than from George Weymouth, who is said to have brought pines back from Maine.) Over the years, Weymouth's heirs planted even more. The third viscount, between 1755 and 1796, "planted, without intermission, at least fifty thousand trees, on an average annually." The trees were never successful as mast trees, but some grew and prospered. Europeans took to the tree and planted it across the continent.

The trees that Clifford Pettis was inspecting were likely cousins of the trees from the Weymouth estate. Due to the success of the replanting programs in America, and the very attractive prices for white pine seedlings in Europe, the United States ordered baby trees by the millions.

When Dr. Perley Spaulding read Clifford Pettis's telegram he had an idea what the swelling might be, and it wasn't good. As soon as was possible, he made the trip to Geneva to have a look at Pettis's pines. It was just as he feared—the trees were infected with blister rust. How many tainted seedlings had been sent out to reforestation efforts, he wondered, before Pettis made his find? The eastern white pine was still a major economic power in many states, and a blight could be truly devastating.

A disease caused by a tiny parasitic fungus, blister rust had been a problem in Europe since at least the 1850s, killing white pines big and small. It dispatched young trees swiftly; larger trees fared better, dying slower and sometimes even surviving the disease. The parasite looked for weakness in the trees, scrapes and wounds and holes, or infiltrated through tiny openings in the cuticles of the needles, where the pines do their breathing, taking in carbon dioxide and letting out oxygen.

White pine blister rust is unusual in that the parasite needs not a single host tree—but two host trees of different species—in order to spread. Two white pines could sit closely together in a forest, touching even, and the disease would not be able to move from one to the next. But place a host tree—or bush—in between the two trees and it will quickly spread.

The yellow parasite seems to like currant and gooseberry bushes, members of the ribes genus, but it does them little harm, only using the fruit trees as a launching pad from which to attack neighboring white pines. And it only likes white pines— eastern, western, and sugar—and has no interest in any other pine family conifers.

Dr. Spaulding knew an epidemic of white pine blister rust could be as catastrophic to the country's valuable pineries—estimated to be valued at more than $1 billion in 1919—as a wildfire.

Foresters combating the spread of blister rust had one factor in their favor: the disease multiplies in an unusual way. It spreads from a white pine to ribes, then from ribes to ribes, then back to the white pine. After it mutates long enough on the pine, its blisters erupt, sending bright orange spores flying. These land on ribes, where they grow and develop new and different spores, which then bombard the towering evergreen next door. The ribe family is found throughout the nation, with more than sixty-five varieties available to harbor parasites. But while the spores that spread from pine to ribe are quite capable and tough, able to be blown like pollen across large stretches of forest, grabbing on to bushes as they go, the spores that travel from bush to tree are much heavier—yet more sensitive. They're capable of going only a few hundred yards.

The secret for foresters was to simply find ribe bushes in pine forests and remove them—and they had much of the year to do it. Blister rust rarely survives winter on a gooseberry or currant bush, and only thrives when leaves are full.

The pines, however, suffer year round. The disease infects them through their needles and permeates into the cells of the branches, killing off limbs one by one. Trunks sport big ugly yellow blisters, oozing spores—the parasite can girdle a tree with the same deadly efficiency as a woodsman angry at a distant monarch. Because the disease isn't native to North America, the trees have no built-in resistance and they succumb readily.

According to the U.S. Forest Service, white pine blister rust was first noticed in, of all places, the Baltic forests of Russia, infecting the same forests that once provided England's Royal Navy with masts. From there it was a steady march west across the continent before it started showing up in nurseries in Germany. It found plenty of ribes plants along the way—Europeans cultivated gooseberries and particularly black currant plants, which were extremely popular to grow in the backyard and make into jams, purees, syrups, and cordials. One survey, conducted in the first few years of the twentieth century, showed that 95 percent of Europeans living in rural areas grew black currants.

It quickly became very clear that this deadly yellow fungus was the reason that the eastern white pine was exclusively a North American phenomenon. Though many in England, France, and Germany had attempted to import it to Europe, the tree never succeeded there. Whole plantations fell to blister rust, and the Europeans were reluctant to start eradicating the problem because they valued the ribes family more—all those cultivated black currants—than they did the stately *Pinus strobus*.

In the United States, of course, that wasn't the case. The eastern white pine, the tree that built a nation, was infinitely more important than little gooseberry bushes. Americans were happy to tear ribes apart, ripping them up by the roots, in order to save the pines.

Once foresters knew the yellow signs to look for, they began to find it all over.

After Clifford Petiss found those two yellowed pines in 1909, the disease was discovered across New York State, and it began to travel outward. Scientists from the U.S. Department of Agriculture's Office of Forest Pathology were the point men at the federal level, and they began to mobilize an attempt to quarantine the disease, just as their colleagues at the U.S. Centers for Disease Control might in the face of a viral epidemic. They discovered to their great dismay that in 1909 millions of seedlings had been imported from the J. HeinSohne nursery in Halstenbeck, Germany, which was known to be contaminated. These potentially blighted trees were sent to 226 different communities across the country. Millions more had come in from stock in France that was suspected to be infected.

Scientists and foresters began to spread out, inspecting nurseries. Trees bearing the ugly yellow hallmark of the disease were found in Massachusetts, New Hampshire, Vermont, Connecticut, Pennsylvania, Ohio, and Indiana, and it had made it as far north as the Canadian provinces of Quebec and Ontario.

It would be virtually impossible to intercept all those trees before they made it into the ground.

Foresters furiously began to assemble teams to try and save the pines they could, using fungicides to attempt to kill the parasite and amputating limbs to try and keep individual trees alive. They deployed more than eleven thousand CCC corpsmen to the national forests, destroying all the ribes they could find, and began a new Blister Rust Control (BRC) program on the national level. (The federal government placed a ban on the importation of new seedlings from Europe; the 1912 Plant Quarantine Act was passed in response to the blister rust threat.)

Despite the best efforts of forest pathologists, the yellow blight began to spread. By the 1920s, the forests of New Hampshire, the pineries that once produced so many masts for the Royal Navy, were heavily blighted. Scientists estimated that roughly half of the eastern white pines in the Granite State had been affected; within thirty years, the infection destroyed more than seven billion board feet of lumber. Newspaper headlines decried the "evil" disease. Massachusetts, New Hampshire, and Maine all banned the cultivation of ribes plants to try and stem the tide. Even so, white pine blister rust was exploding in yellow spore clouds all across North America, working its way into the forests of thirty-eight states, killing trees as it climbed hillsides and dropped into moist hollows. Whole woodlands felt its effect, not just the trees themselves, as the parasite despoiled the landscape. All the creatures and plants that relied on pines suffered, like the chipmunks and squirrels that eat their seeds, the chickadees that make their homes in them, the woodpeckers that find meals inside, the deer that nibbles its branches, the whitetail rabbits that use its needles for cover.

Eradication efforts paid off, greatly slowing the blister rust epidemic, and they were helped along by the maturation of trees. When eastern white pines grow tall they lift their branches out of the danger zone of infection by blister rust. Older trees tend to die less frequently. Ribes in the northeast went into a decline. And timber companies and landowners planted white pine under canopies, which limits the moisture below the trees that could become a breeding ground for the fungus. Foresters had the disease under control enough that it was no longer a significant threat to lumber production.

Or so they thought.

In 2011, a century after Clifford Pettis noticed the yellow growth on his white pine seedlings, another Cornell student made another startling blister rust discovery—like every good parasite, the disease was mutating. A new strain was infecting ribes plants that had been previously thought to be immune—and had found other hosts outside the ribe family, like Indian paintbrush and snapdragon. Just as they did in 1909, foresters and pathologists scrambled to meet the new threat.

New Hampshire's forest health program manager, Kyle Lombard, told the *Star Tribune* the state was taking white pine blister rust very seriously. "Pine is still the king in New Hampshire," he said. "We grow and cut more pine in New Hampshire than any other tree species."

Despite threats from foreign monarchs, rapacious timber cutters, epic wildfires, and parasitic fungi, pine is still king. Quintessentially American, it still towers over eastern forests, standing sentinel above many of our favorite places. Four hundred years after Europeans planted plantations in New England to harvest the noble evergreen, *Pinus strobus* holds its value as a commercial commodity. As Kevin Hancock of Hancock Lumber says: "It's still considered to be a premium, unique, beautiful product that is rare by global standards."

In addition to being fashioned into innumerable lumber and wood products, the eastern white pine has served as the White House Christmas tree; it went into Leo Fender's first Telecaster; it's made into teas and tinctures, vitamins and salves; it's the state tree of Maine and Michigan, sits atop the Massachusetts State House in the form of a pine cone, and is front and center on the flag of Vermont; it makes appearances at every New England Revolution soccer match on the flag of New England; is sculpted into bonsais, adds aroma to soaps, and flavors drinkable vinegar.

And the reign of the tree doesn't look likely to change. According to the Northeastern Lumber Manufacturers Association, the eastern white pine is selling in record numbers. Between January and June 2016 alone, 471 million board feet made its way into the marketplace. Exports, too, were up, with more than 4 million board feet sent overseas. Almost two thirds of this lumber went to

China, but the United Kingdom was next on the list, accounting for about a half million board feet. It's a far cry from the days when the woods of Maine and Minnesota and Michigan produced board feet by the billions.

But tiny little white pine seedlings push their heads up into a different world today.

Endnotes

Preface

1. Saijo, Albert, "Me, Muir, and Sierra Nevada," in *Reinhabiting a Separate Country: A Bioregional Anthology of Northern California*, edited by Peter Berg. San Francisco: Planet Drum Foundation, 1978, p. 55.

Introduction: White Pine Riot

1. Little, William, *The History of Weare, New Hampshire*. Lowell, MA: S. W. Huse and Co., 1888, p. 191.
2. Ibid., p. 189.
3. Ibid.
4. Ibid.
5. O'Callaghan, E. B., *Documentary History of the State of New York*, Vol. 4. Albany, NY: Charles Van Benthuysen, Public Printer, 1851, p. 632.
6. Charter of Massachusetts Bay, 1691.
7. Little, *History of Weare*, p. 188.
8. Browne, George Waldo, *The History of Hillsborough, New Hampshire, 1735–1921*. Manchester, NH: John B. Clarke Company, Printers, 1921, p. 100.
9. Little, *History of Weare*, p. 190.

Chapter 1: The Bark Eaters

1. Alexie, Sherman. *The Lone Ranger and Tonto Fistfight in Heaven*. New York: Open Road Media, 1993, p. 29.
2. Marching.com. Macy's Thanksgiving Day Parade Lineup and Parade Route, retrieved 1/20/16.
3. Indiancountrytodaymedianetwork.com, 11/23/11, retrieved 1/20/16.
4. Parker, Arthur C., and William Nelson Fenton, *Parker on the Iroquois*. Syracuse, NY: Syracuse University Press, 1968, p. 154.
5. Gibbings, W. W., *North American Indian: Folklore and Legends*. London: W. W. Gibbings, 1890, p. 13.

6. Olcott, Frances Jenkins. *The Red Indian Fairy Book*. Boston and New York: Houghton Mifflin Co., 1917, p. 236.

7. Ibid., p. 9.

8. Smith, Huron H., *Ethnobotany of the Ojibwe Indians*. Milwaukee, WI: Bulletin of the Public Museum of the City of Milwaukee, 1932, p. 406.

9. http://www.ncnatural.com/NCNatural/trees/bigtrees.html, retrieved 1/20/16.

Chapter 2: The Forest for the Trees

1. Rosier, James, *A True Relation of Captain George Weymouth His Voyage, Made This Present Yeere, 1605: In the Discoverie of the North Part of Virginia.* Wisconsin Historical Society Digital Library and Archives, 2003, p. 382

2. Ibid., p. 362.

3. Ibid., p. 363.

4. Ibid., p. 364.

5. Ibid.

6. Ibid., p. 366.

7. Ibid., p. 385.

8. http://www.americanjourneys.org/aj-041/summary, retrieved 1/15/16.

9. Rosier, *A True Relation of Captain George Weymouth*, p. 365.

10. Williamson, James, A. D., Litt., *The Voyages of the Cabots & the English Discovery of North America under Henry VII & VIII*. London: The Argonaut Press, 1929.

11. http://www.columbia.edu/~lmg21/ash3002y/earlyac99/documents/verrazan.htm, retrieved 1/18/16.

12. Ibid.

13. http://www.bairnet.org/potw/gomez99/gomez.htm, retrieved 1/17/16.

14. Hakluyt, Richard, *The Principal Navigations, Voyages, Traffiques and Discoveries of the English Nation, VIII*. New York: Macmillan Co., 1904, p. 139.

15. Carman, Harry J. *A History of the American People: Vol 1 to 1865*. New York: Alfred A. Knopf, 1952, p. 16.

16. Poor, John A., *A Vindication of the Claims of Sir Ferdinando Gorges as the Father of English Colonization in America*. New York: D. Appleton and Company, 1862, p. 30.

17. Ballard, Rev. Edward, *Memorial Volume of the Popham Celebration, August 29, 1862*. Portland, ME: Bailey and Noyes, 1863, p. 31.

18. Ibid.

19. Schneider, Jim, and Holly Rubin, *The Ancestry of J. G. Williams and Ursula Miller*. Authors, 2013, p. 24.

Chapter 3: Trees across the Seas

1. Poor, John Alfred, *The First Colonization of New England*. New York: Anson DF Publisher and Bookseller, 1863, p. 52.

2. Everett, Edward, *An Oration Delivered at Plymouth, December 22, 1824.* Boston: Cummings, Hilliard, and Co., 1825, p. 14.

3. Rice, Douglas Walthew,. *The Life and Achievements of Sir John Popham, 1531–1607, Leading to the Establishment of the First English Colony in America.* Madison and Teaneck, NJ: Fairleigh Dickinson University Press, 2005, p. 235.

4. Brown, Alexander, *The First Republic in America.* Boston: Houghton Mifflin and Co., 1898, p. 3.

5. Ballard, Edward, ed. *Memorial Volume of the Popham Celebration, August 29, 1862.* Portland, Maine: Bailey & Noyes, 1863, p. 67.

6. http://nationalhumanitiescenter.org/pds/amerbegin/exploration/text5/hakluyt.pdf, retrieved 11/1/16.

7. Beers, George Louis, *Origins of the British Colonial System, 1578–1660.* New York: Macmillan, 1908, p. 66.

8. Poor, John A., *English Colonization in America: A Vindication of the Claims of Sir Ferdinando Gorges as the Father of Colonization in America.* New York: D. Appleton and Co., 1862, p. 129.

9. Ballard, *Memorial Volume*, p. 43.

10. Sewall, Rufus King, *Ancient Dominions of Maine.* Bath: Elisha Clark and Co., 1859, p. 81.

11. Baxter, James Phinney, *Sir Ferdinando Gorges and His Province of Maine*, Vol. 1. Boston: The Prince Society, 1890, p. 77.

12. Collections of the Maine Historical Society, Vol. 3. Portland, ME: Published for the Society, 1847, p. 299.

13. Collections and Proceedings of the Maine Historical Society, Second Series Vol. 2, 1891, p. 281.

14. Brown, Alexander, *The Genesis of the United States.* Boston: Houghton Mifflin and Co., 1890, p. 146.

15. Ibid., p. 152.

16. Benians, E. A., *Captain John Smith: Travels, History of Virginia.* New York: Cambridge University Press, 2012, p. 96.

17. Ibid., p.100.

18. Ibid., p. 105.

19. Collections of the Maine Historical Society, Vol. 2. Portland, ME: Published for the Society, 1847, p. 23.

20. Collections and Proceedings of the Maine Historical Society, Second Series Vol. 2, 1891, p. 282.

21. Burrage, Henry Sweetser, *Beginnings of Colonial Maine, 1602–1658.* "Printed for the State," 1914, p. 88.

Chapter 4: The Dominion of New England

1. Webb, Stephen Saunders, *Lord Churchill's Coup: The AngloAmerican Empire and the Glorious Revolution Reconsidered.* Syracuse, NY: Syracuse University Press, 1998, pp. 86–87.

2. Peterson, Henry, *Dulcibell: A Tale of Old Salem*. Philadelphia: John C. Winston, Co., 1907, p. 252.

3. Palfrey, John, *History of New England During the Stuart Dynasty*. Boston: Little, Brown, 1864, p. 586.

4. *Edward Randolph: Including His Letters and Official Papers from the New England, Middle, and Southern Colonies in America*, Vol. 3. Boston: Prince Society, 1899, p. 70.

5. Ibid., p. 4.

6. Ibid., p. 6.

7. Washburn, Emory, *Sketches of the Judicial History of Massachusetts, from 1630 to the Revolution, 1775*. Boston: Charles C. Little and James Brown, 1840, p. 129.

8. Calendar of State Papers, Colonial Series, America and West Indies, 1899, pp. 614–615.

9. Brittain, Alfred and Reed, George. *The History of North America, Vol. I: Discovery and Exploration*. Philadelphia: George Barrie and Sons, 1903, p. 466.

10. Calendar of State Papers, Vol. 5, p. 100.

11. Rutkow, Eric, *American Canopy: Trees, Forests, and the Making of a Nation*. New York: Scribner, 2012.

12. Defebaugh, *History of the Lumber Industry of America*, Vol. 2, p. 6.

13. Hills, Richard Leslie, *Power from Wind: A History of Windmill Technology*. New York: Cambridge University Press, p. 166.

14. Morton, Thomas, *The New English Canaan*. Boston: Prince Society, 1883, p. 184.

15. Calendar of State Papers, Vol. 6, p. 156.

16. Palfrey, John Gorham, *History of New England*. Boston: Little, Brown Publishers, 1897, p. 365.

17. *Edward Randolph: Including His Letters and Official Papers from the New England, Middle, and Southern Colonies in America*, Vol. 25. Boston: Prince Society, 1898, p. 248.

18. Rutkow, *American Canopy*, p. 25.

19. "New England Masts and the King's Navy," *New England Quarterly*, 1939, pp. 4–18.

20. The Council of State to the Governors and Commissioners of the United Colonies of New England, Calendar of State Papers, Vol. 119, Sect. 202.

21. http://www.pepysdiary.com/diary/1666/12/, retrieved 11/4/16.

22. *Diary and Correspondence of Samuel Pepys*, Vol. 3. New York: Bigelow, Brown and Co. Inc., 1920, p. 35.

23. Sloane, Eric, *A Reverence for Wood*. New York: Wilfred Funk, 1965, p. 75.

24. http://oll.libertyfund.org/pages/1661-act-of-the-general-court-of-mass, retrieved 10/14/16.

25. http://www.usahistory.info/NewEngland/Edmund-Andros.html, retrieved 10/21/16.

Chapter 5: The Case of Cooke

1. *The American Historical Review*, Vol. 9, No. 2 (January 1904), pp. 371–375.

2. Brown, Richard Maxwell, *Strain of Violence: Historical Studies of American Violence and Vigilantism*. New York: Oxford University Press, 1975, p. 52.

3. Anno Regni, Annae Reginae,
   Magna Britannia, Francia, & Hibernia,
   Nono, London,
   Printed by the Assigns of Thomas Newcomb,
   and Henry Hills, decea'd; Printers to the
   Queens most Excellent Majesty. 1711. [Excerpted from the White Pines Act.]

4. Sanborn, Edwin David. *History of New Hampshire from its First Discovery to 1830*. Manchester, New Hampshire: John B. Clarke, 1875, p. 32.

5. Faculty of Political Science, Columbia University, eds., *Studies in History, Economics, and Public Law*. New York: Columbia University Press, 1920, p. 43.

6. James, Bartlett Burleigh, *History of North America*, Vol. 5. London: George Barrie and Sons, 1904, p. 341.

7. Proceedings of the Massachusetts Historical Society, Third Series, Vol. 78, 1966, p. 136.

8. Baxter, James Phinney, ed. *Maine Historical Society. Documentary History of the State of Maine Vol 9*. Portland: Lefavor Company, 1869, p. 415.

9. Ibid., p. 416.

10. Ibid., p. 425.

11. Ibid., p. 425.

12. Albion, Robert Greenhalgh, *Forests and Sea Power*. Boston: Harvard University Press, 1926, p. 256.

13. Report from Gov. Shute to the Board of Trade, B. T. New Eng., X:36.

14. Chalmers, George, *An Introduction to the History of the Revolt of the Colonies*. London: Baker and Galabin, 1782, p. 401.

15. *Documentary History of the State of Maine*, pp. 415–418.

16. Malone, Joseph J., *Pine Trees and Politics: 1691–1775*. Seattle: University of Washington Press, 1965, p. 106.

17. *Documentary History of the State of Maine*, p. 438.

18. Ibid.

19. Lord, Eleanor Louisa. *Industrial Experiments in the British Colonies of North America*. Baltimore: The Johns Hopkins Press, 1898, p. 115.

20. Emory, *Sketches of the Judicial History of Massachusetts*, p. 331.

Chapter 6: The Mast Trade

1. Willcox, William B., ed., *The Papers of Benjamin Franklin*, Vol. 17, January 1 through December 31, 1770. New Haven and London: Yale University Press, 1973, pp. 33–36.

2. *Documentary History of the State of Maine,* Vol. 10, p. 428.

3. Goold, William, *Portland in the Past: With Historical Notes of Old Falmouth.* Falmouth, 1886, pp. 194–195.

4. Pike, Robert E., *Tall Trees, Tough Men.* New York: W. W. Norton Co., 1999, p. 40.

5. Carlton, William R. "New England Masts and the King's Navy." *The New England Quarterly,* vol. 12, no. 1, 1939, pp. 4–18.

6. Frisbee, Oliver, "The Piscataqua Mast Fleet." *The Granite Monthly: A New Hampshire Magazine.* Concord, NH, 1917, p. 19.

7. Rutkow, *American Canopy,* p. 32.

8. Malone, *Pine Trees and Politics.*

9. Ibid.

10. Barry, William David, and Francis W. Peabody, *Tate House: Crown of the Mast Trade.* Portland, ME: National Society of Colonial Dames of America in the State of Maine, 1982, p. 19.

11. www.pepysdiary.com/encyclopedia/1748/, retrieved 10/27/16.

12. Merchant, Carolyn, ed. *Major Problems in American Environmental History,* 2nd Edition, Boston: Houghton Mifflin, 2005, p.88.

13. Barry and Peabody, *Tate House,* p. 14.

14. Albion, *Forests and Sea Power.*

Chapter 7: Woodcutters Revolt

1. Sewall, *Ancient Dominions of Maine,* pp. 327–328.

2. http://www.british-history.ac.uk/cal-state-papers/colonial/america-west-indies/vol37/pp237-251, retrieved 11/4/16.

3. Albion, *Forests and Sea Power,* p. 271.

4. Ibid., p. 272.

5. Ibid., p. 263.

6. Calendar of State Papers Colonial, America and West Indies: Volume 17, 1699 and Addenda 1621–1698. London: His Majesty's Stationery Office, London, 1908. p. 418.

7. Calendar of Treasury Papers, 1720–1728. London: Eyre and Spottiswood, 1889, p. 406.

8. Sewall, *Ancient Dominions of Maine,* p. 260.

9. Ibid.

10. Cushman, David Quimby, *History of Ancient Sheepscot and Newcastle.* Damariscotta, ME: E. Upton and Son Printers, 1882, p. 106.

11. *Documentary History of the State of Maine,* p. 44.

12. Greene, Francis Byron, *History of Boothbay, Southport, and Boothbay Harbor, 1623–1905.* Portland, ME: Loring, 1906, p. 123.

13. Malone, *Pine Trees and Politics,* p. 102.

14. Ibid., p. 104.

15. Cox, Sam, "White Pine Blister Rust: The Story of White Pine, American Revolution, Lumberjacks, and Grizzly Bears." http://www.landscapeimagery .com/wphistory.html. Retrieved 1/17/17.

16. Pike, *Tall Trees, Tough Men*, p. 48.

17. Albion, *Forests and Sea Power*, p. 262.

18. Whiton, John M. *Sketches of the History of New Hampshire, from its Settlement in 1623 to 1833.* Concord: Marsh, Capen, and Lyon, 1834, p. 80.

19. *Documentary History of the State of Maine*, p. 6.

20. Malone, *Pine Trees and Politics*, p. 105.

21. *Documentary History of the State of Maine*, Vol. 11, p. 20.

22. Ibid., p. 39.

23. Dawson, Henry B. *The Historical Magazine and Notes and Queries Concerning the Antiquities, History, and Biography of America*, Vol. 8. Morrisania, NY: Dawson, 1870, p. 15.

24. Ibid.

25. Ibid.

26. Ibid., p. 14.

27. Ibid.

28. Ibid.

29. Ibid., p. 16.

30. Ibid., p. 17.

31. *Documentary History of the State of Maine*, p. 4.

Chapter 8: Tree of Liberty, City of Fire

1. Collections of the Maine Historical Society. Portland, ME: The Society, 1904, p. 209.

2. Sinnett, Reverend Charles N. *Our Thompson Family in Maine, New Hampshire, and the West.* Concord, NH: Rumford Printing Co., 1907, p. 19.

3. Sinnett, p. 21.

4. Collections of the Maine Historical Society, Portland, ME: The Society, 1904, p. 433.

5. Ibid., p. 435.

6. *Documentary History of the State of Maine*, Vol. 14. Portland, ME: Bailey and Noyes, 1910, p. 246.

7. Ibid., p. 287.

8. Albion, *Forests and Sea Power*, p. 263.

9. *The Journals of Each Provincial Congress of Massachusetts in 1774 and 1775*, Dutton and Wentworth Printers to the State, 1838, p. 218.

10. *The New England Historical and Genealogical Register*, Vol. 12. Boston: Samuel G. Drake, Publisher, 1858, p. 318.

11. *The New England Historical and Genealogical Register*, Vol. 27, Boston: Heritage Books, p. 261.

12. Goold, William. *Portland in the Past, with Historical Notes of Old Falmouth.* Portland: B. Thurston and Co, 1886, p. 342.

13. http://www.legacy-america.net/2014/10/18/day-history-october-18-1775 -burning-falmouth-maine-fanning-flames-revolution/, retrieved 11/1/16.

14. Willis, William, *The History of Portland, from 1632 to 1864.* Portland, ME: Bailey and Noyes, 1865, p. 517.

15. Ibid.

16. Collections of the Maine Historical Society, Vol. 5, p. 448.

17. Letter from Mowatt to Vice Admiral Graves, October 19, 1775, Maine Historical Society.

Chapter 9: Revolution Comes

1. Hubert, Patricia M., *Major Philip M. Ulmer: A Hero of the American Revolution.* Charleston, SC: History Press, 2014, p. 131.

2. *Fishermen's Voice*, April 2001.

3. Miller, Nathan, *Sea of Glory: The Continental Navy Fights for Independence, 1775–1783.* New York: David McKay, 1974, p. 49.

4. http://www.ushistory.org/declaration/document/, retrieved 11/4/16.

5. www.drjosephwarren.com, retrieved 11/1/16.

6. Extracts Relating to the Origin of the American Navy. New England Historic Genealogical Society, Boston:1890, p. 13.

7. http://www.americanlibertyassociation.com/2013/10/22/appeal-to-heaven/, retrieved 10/22/16.

8. Albion, *Forests and Sea Power*, p. 276.

9. Ibid., p. 278.

10. Cushman, *History of Ancient Sheepscot and Newcastle*, pp. 212–213.

11. Albion, *Forests and Sea Power*, p. 298.

12. *The Scots Magazine*, Vol. 50. Edinburgh: Sands, Brymer, Murray, and Cochran, 1788, p. 450.

Chapter 10: The Aroostook War

1. Maine Council, *Aroostook War: Historical Sketch and Roster of Commissioned Officers and Enlisted Men*, Augusta, ME: Kennebec Journal Printers, 1904, p. 15.

2. Seager, Robert II, *From the Papers of Henry Clay: The Whig Leader, January 1, 1837–December 31, 1843*, Vol. 9. Lexington: University Press of Kentucky, 1988, p. 291.

3. *Journal of the House of Commons*, Vol. 47, 1803, p. 360.

4. Thoreau, Henry David, *The Maine Woods.* Boston and New York: The Houghton Mifflin Co., 1892, p. 83.

5. Ibid., p. 111.

6. Ibid., p. 45.

7. Rogers, D. Laurence, *Paul Bunyan: How a Terrible Timber Feller Became a Legend*, Bay City, MI: Historical Press, 1993.
8. Ibid.

Chapter 13: If a Tree Falls
1. Leopold, Aldo, *A Sand County Almanac, and Sketches Here and There, 1948*. New York: Oxford University Press, 1987, p. 81.

Chapter 14: Snags
1. "The National Parks and Forest Reservations," speech by John Muir, *Sierra Club Bulletin*, Vol. 1, no. 7, January 1896, pp. 282–283.

Index

ABOUT THE AUTHOR

Bestselling Maine author **Andrew Vietze** has been called "an excellent New England historian" by the *Kennebec Journal* and has won several awards for his history writing. The former managing editor of *Down East: The Magazine of Maine*, he's the author of six books, including *Boon Island* and *Becoming Teddy Roosevelt*, both of which were regional bestsellers, won Independent Publisher Book Awards, and were finalists for Book of the Year Awards (ForeWord Reviews). *Becoming Teddy Roosevelt* was also honored by decree of the Maine State Legislature as an example of what Maine writing should be and has become part of a conservation program for middle schoolers at Coastal Maine Botanical Gardens (called the nation's best public garden by TripAdvisor); *Boon Island* was called "a maritime whodunit rife with twist and turns and high drama" by *Publishers Weekly* and "superb. . . both well-researched history and a page-turning mystery that begs to be a motion picture" by the *Portsmouth Herald*. The book has attracted much attention from Hollywood and was featured on the Travel Channel show, *Monumental Mysteries*, in January of 2014.

As a journalist, Vietze has won awards for history writing from the International Regional Magazine Association. His work has appeared in a wide array of print and online publications, including: the *New York Times*' LifeWire, *Time Out New York*, Weather.com's "Forecast Earth," *AMC Outdoors, Explore, Big Sky Journal, Crawdaddy!, Popmatters, Offshore*, and the *Maine Times*, and he has twice won awards for history writing from the International Regional Magazine Association.

A Registered Maine Guide, Andrew Vietze had a tree fort in a tall old pine during his childhood and used to walk from one tree to the next in the forest canopy twenty feet above the ground. He spends half the year working as a seasonal ranger in Baxter State Park, stationed at an old sporting camp called Twin Pines.